THIS BOOK BELONGS TO:

- -

- -

INDEX OF BATCHES

BATCH	TEST DATE	RATING	NOTES

CANDLE CREATION LOG

DATE CREATED

CANDLE NAME

INGREDIENTS	AMOUNT	METHOD SUMMARY

OILS AND SCENTS	MOLD & FINISH

OVERALL RATING

○ 1   ○ 2   ○ 3   ○ 4   ○ 5   ○ 6   ○ 7   ○ 8   ○ 9   ○ 10

CANDLE MAKING LOGBOOK

DATE		BATCH	

NOTES

CANDLE TYPE

○ PILLAR	○ GEL		
○ VOTIVE	○ CONTAINER	TYPE:	SIZE:
○ TART/MELT	○ OTHER		

WAX TYPE

○ PARAFFIN	○ BEESWAX
○ SOY	○ GEL
○ PALM	○ OTHER

AMBIENT ROOM TEMP			
WAX BRAND			
QUANTITY			
MELT TEMP		POUR TEMP	
FRAGRANCE USED			
AMOUNT USED		POUR TEMP	
DYE TYPE		COLOR	
AMOUNT USED		TEMP ADDED	
WICK TYPE		SIZE	
CORE MATERIAL		# OF WICKS USED	
MOLD OR CONTAINER	○ MOLD ○ CONTAINER		
MOLD RELEASE USED	○ YES ○ NO		
WAS CONTAINER WARMED	○ YES ○ NO		
COOLING TIME		CURING TIME	

PROJECT		CREATED FOR			
DATE STARTED		DATE COMPLETED		RANK	/10
CANDLE TYPE	○ GLASSSES ○ JARS ○ OTHERS:				
WAX TYPE & BRAND		Q-TY			
POUR TEMP		MELT TEMP			
ADDITIVES USED					
SUPPLIES NEEDED					
COSTS					

INGREDIENTS	NAME / TYPE / BRAND	AMOUNT USED / SIZE	NOTES (TEMP/COLOR/ETC)
FRAGRANCE OIL			
DYE			
WICK			

AMBIENT ROOM TEMP		○ CONTAINER ○ MOLD		NUMBER OF POURS	
COOLING TIME		FINAL PRODUCT THROW	1 2 3 4 5	HOT THROW	1 2 3 4 5
MELT POOL		DIFFICULTY	○ EASY ○ MODERATE ○ CHALLENGING		
NOTES					

CANDLE MAKING LOGBOOK

NAME OF CANDLE		DATE MADE	
SIZE OF CANDLES		WAX TOTAL	
NUMBER OF CANDLES		FRAGRANCE TOTAL	
ROOM TEMPERATURE		FRAGRANCE PERCENTAGE	

WAX	AMOUNTS	VENDOR / BATCH #
○		
○		
○		
○		
○		
○		
○		
○		
○		

FRAGRANCE	VANILLIN?	AMOUNTS	VENDOR / BATCH #
○	○ Y ○ N		
○	○ Y ○ N		
○	○ Y ○ N		
○	○ Y ○ N		
○	○ Y ○ N		
○	○ Y ○ N		
○	○ Y ○ N		
○	○ Y ○ N		

JAR / VESSEL / MOLD	WIDTH	HEIGHT
VENDOR		

WICK	QUANTITY	HEIGHT
VENDOR		

COLORANT	AMOUNTS	VENDOR / BATCH #
○		
○		
○		
○		
○		
○		

ACTIVITIES	AMOUNTS	VENDOR / BATCH #
○		
○		
○		
○		
○		
○		

THE WAX IS HEATED TO WHAT TEMPERATURE?	
THE FRAGRANCE IS ADDED AT WHAT TEMPERATURE?	
THE FRAGRANCE IS STIRRED IN THE WAX FOR HOW LONG?	
THE WAX IS POURED AT WHAT TEMPERATURE?	

NOTES

TEST BURN A

DATE		START TIME		END TIME	
ROOM SIZE		DAYS / WEEKS CURED			
CT	○ FAINT ○ DECENT ○ GOOD ○ GREAT ○ AMAZING			WICK TRIMMED	○ Y ○ N
OBSERVATIONS DURING THE FIRST BURN TEST					
RESULTS AFTER THE BURN					
HT	○ FAINT ○ DECENT ○ GOOD ○ GREAT ○ AMAZING			TOTAL BURN TIME	
WICK	○ OVER WICKED / TOO BIG		○ PROPERLY WICKED	○ UNDER WICKED / TOO SMALL	

TEST BURN B

DATE		START TIME		END TIME	
ROOM SIZE		DAYS / WEEKS CURED			
CT	○ FAINT ○ DECENT ○ GOOD ○ GREAT ○ AMAZING			WICK TRIMMED	○ Y ○ N
OBSERVATIONS DURING THE FIRST BURN TEST					
RESULTS AFTER THE BURN					
HT	○ FAINT ○ DECENT ○ GOOD ○ GREAT ○ AMAZING			TOTAL BURN TIME	
WICK	○ OVER WICKED / TOO BIG		○ PROPERLY WICKED	○ UNDER WICKED / TOO SMALL	

TEST BURN C

DATE		START TIME		END TIME	
ROOM SIZE		DAYS / WEEKS CURED			
CT	○ FAINT ○ DECENT ○ GOOD ○ GREAT ○ AMAZING			WICK TRIMMED	○ Y ○ N

OBSERVATIONS DURING THE FIRST BURN TEST

RESULTS AFTER THE BURN

HT	○ FAINT ○ DECENT ○ GOOD ○ GREAT ○ AMAZING	TOTAL BURN TIME	
WICK	○ OVER WICKED / TOO BIG	○ PROPERLY WICKED	○ UNDER WICKED / TOO SMALL

TEST BURN D

DATE		START TIME		END TIME	
ROOM SIZE		DAYS / WEEKS CURED			
CT	○ FAINT ○ DECENT ○ GOOD ○ GREAT ○ AMAZING			WICK TRIMMED	○ Y ○ N

OBSERVATIONS DURING THE FIRST BURN TEST

RESULTS AFTER THE BURN

HT	○ FAINT ○ DECENT ○ GOOD ○ GREAT ○ AMAZING	TOTAL BURN TIME	
WICK	○ OVER WICKED / TOO BIG	○ PROPERLY WICKED	○ UNDER WICKED / TOO SMALL

CANDLE CREATION LOG

DATE CREATED

CANDLE NAME

INGREDIENTS	AMOUNT	METHOD SUMMARY

OILS AND SCENTS	MOLD & FINISH

OVERALL RATING

○ 1 ○ 2 ○ 3 ○ 4 ○ 5 ○ 6 ○ 7 ○ 8 ○ 9 ○ 10

CANDLE MAKING LOGBOOK

DATE		BATCH	

NOTES

CANDLE TYPE

○ PILLAR	○ GEL
○ VOTIVE	○ CONTAINER TYPE: SIZE:
○ TART/MELT	○ OTHER

WAX TYPE

○ PARAFFIN	○ BEESWAX
○ SOY	○ GEL
○ PALM	○ OTHER

AMBIENT ROOM TEMP			
WAX BRAND			
QUANTITY			
MELT TEMP		POUR TEMP	
FRAGRANCE USED			
AMOUNT USED		POUR TEMP	
DYE TYPE		COLOR	
AMOUNT USED		TEMP ADDED	
WICK TYPE		SIZE	
CORE MATERIAL		# OF WICKS USED	
MOLD OR CONTAINER	○ MOLD ○ CONTAINER		
MOLD RELEASE USED	○ YES ○ NO		
WAS CONTAINER WARMED	○ YES ○ NO		
COOLING TIME		CURING TIME	

PROJECT		CREATED FOR			
DATE STARTED		DATE COMPLETED		RANK	/10
CANDLE TYPE	○ GLASSSES ○ JARS ○ OTHERS:				
WAX TYPE & BRAND		Q-TY			
POUR TEMP		MELT TEMP			
ADDITIVES USED					
SUPPLIES NEEDED					
COSTS					

INGREDIENTS	NAME / TYPE / BRAND	AMOUNT USED / SIZE	NOTES (TEMP/COLOR/ETC)
FRAGRANCE OIL			
DYE			
WICK			

AMBIENT ROOM TEMP		○ CONTAINER ○ MOLD		NUMBER OF POURS	
COOLING TIME		FINAL PRODUCT THROW	1 2 3 4 5	HOT THROW	1 2 3 4 5
MELT POOL		DIFFICULTY	○ EASY ○ MODERATE ○ CHALLENGING		

NOTES

CANDLE MAKING LOGBOOK

NAME OF CANDLE		DATE MADE	
SIZE OF CANDLES		WAX TOTAL	
NUMBER OF CANDLES		FRAGRANCE TOTAL	
ROOM TEMPERATURE		FRAGRANCE PERCENTAGE	

WAX	AMOUNTS	VENDOR / BATCH #
○		
○		
○		
○		
○		
○		
○		
○		
○		

FRAGRANCE	VANILLIN?	AMOUNTS	VENDOR / BATCH #
○	○ Y ○ N		
○	○ Y ○ N		
○	○ Y ○ N		
○	○ Y ○ N		
○	○ Y ○ N		
○	○ Y ○ N		
○	○ Y ○ N		
○	○ Y ○ N		

JAR / VESSEL / MOLD	WIDTH	HEIGHT
VENDOR		

WICK	QUANTITY	HEIGHT
VENDOR		

COLORANT	AMOUNTS	VENDOR / BATCH #
○		
○		
○		
○		
○		
○		

ACTIVITIES	AMOUNTS	VENDOR / BATCH #
○		
○		
○		
○		
○		
○		

THE WAX IS HEATED TO WHAT TEMPERATURE?	
THE FRAGRANCE IS ADDED AT WHAT TEMPERATURE?	
THE FRAGRANCE IS STIRRED IN THE WAX FOR HOW LONG?	
THE WAX IS POURED AT WHAT TEMPERATURE?	

NOTES

TEST BURN A

DATE		START TIME		END TIME	
ROOM SIZE		DAYS / WEEKS CURED			
CT	○ FAINT ○ DECENT ○ GOOD ○ GREAT ○ AMAZING			WICK TRIMMED	○ Y ○ N

OBSERVATIONS DURING THE FIRST BURN TEST

RESULTS AFTER THE BURN

HT	○ FAINT ○ DECENT ○ GOOD ○ GREAT ○ AMAZING	TOTAL BURN TIME	
WICK	○ OVER WICKED / TOO BIG ○ PROPERLY WICKED		○ UNDER WICKED / TOO SMALL

TEST BURN B

DATE		START TIME		END TIME	
ROOM SIZE		DAYS / WEEKS CURED			
CT	○ FAINT ○ DECENT ○ GOOD ○ GREAT ○ AMAZING			WICK TRIMMED	○ Y ○ N

OBSERVATIONS DURING THE FIRST BURN TEST

RESULTS AFTER THE BURN

HT	○ FAINT ○ DECENT ○ GOOD ○ GREAT ○ AMAZING	TOTAL BURN TIME	
WICK	○ OVER WICKED / TOO BIG ○ PROPERLY WICKED		○ UNDER WICKED / TOO SMALL

TEST BURN C

DATE		START TIME		END TIME	
ROOM SIZE		DAYS / WEEKS CURED			
CT	○ FAINT ○ DECENT ○ GOOD ○ GREAT ○ AMAZING			WICK TRIMMED	○ Y ○ N

OBSERVATIONS DURING THE FIRST BURN TEST

_____

_____

_____

RESULTS AFTER THE BURN

_____

_____

_____

HT	○ FAINT ○ DECENT ○ GOOD ○ GREAT ○ AMAZING	TOTAL BURN TIME	
WICK	○ OVER WICKED / TOO BIG ○ PROPERLY WICKED	○ UNDER WICKED / TOO SMALL	

TEST BURN D

DATE		START TIME		END TIME	
ROOM SIZE		DAYS / WEEKS CURED			
CT	○ FAINT ○ DECENT ○ GOOD ○ GREAT ○ AMAZING			WICK TRIMMED	○ Y ○ N

OBSERVATIONS DURING THE FIRST BURN TEST

_____

_____

_____

RESULTS AFTER THE BURN

_____

_____

_____

HT	○ FAINT ○ DECENT ○ GOOD ○ GREAT ○ AMAZING	TOTAL BURN TIME	
WICK	○ OVER WICKED / TOO BIG ○ PROPERLY WICKED	○ UNDER WICKED / TOO SMALL	

CANDLE CREATION LOG

DATE CREATED

CANDLE NAME

INGREDIENTS	AMOUNT	METHOD SUMMARY

OILS AND SCENTS		MOLD & FINISH

OVERALL RATING

○ 1   ○ 2   ○ 3   ○ 4   ○ 5   ○ 6   ○ 7   ○ 8   ○ 9   ○ 10

CANDLE MAKING LOGBOOK

DATE		BATCH	

NOTES

CANDLE TYPE

○ PILLAR	○ GEL
○ VOTIVE	○ CONTAINER TYPE: SIZE:
○ TART/MELT	○ OTHER

WAX TYPE

○ PARAFFIN	○ BEESWAX
○ SOY	○ GEL
○ PALM	○ OTHER

AMBIENT ROOM TEMP			
WAX BRAND			
QUANTITY			
MELT TEMP		POUR TEMP	
FRAGRANCE USED			
AMOUNT USED		POUR TEMP	
DYE TYPE		COLOR	
AMOUNT USED		TEMP ADDED	
WICK TYPE		SIZE	
CORE MATERIAL		# OF WICKS USED	
MOLD OR CONTAINER	○ MOLD ○ CONTAINER		
MOLD RELEASE USED	○ YES ○ NO		
WAS CONTAINER WARMED	○ YES ○ NO		
COOLING TIME		CURING TIME	

PROJECT		CREATED FOR			
DATE STARTED		DATE COMPLETED		RANK	/10
CANDLE TYPE	○ GLASSSES ○ JARS ○ OTHERS:				
WAX TYPE & BRAND		Q-TY			
POUR TEMP		MELT TEMP			
ADDITIVES USED					
SUPPLIES NEEDED					
COSTS					

INGREDIENTS	NAME / TYPE / BRAND	AMOUNT USED / SIZE	NOTES (TEMP/COLOR/ETC)
FRAGRANCE OIL			
DYE			
WICK			

AMBIENT ROOM TEMP		○ CONTAINER ○ MOLD		NUMBER OF POURS	
COOLING TIME		FINAL PRODUCT THROW	1 2 3 4 5	HOT THROW	1 2 3 4 5
MELT POOL		DIFFICULTY	○ EASY ○ MODERATE ○ CHALLENGING		

NOTES

CANDLE MAKING LOGBOOK

NAME OF CANDLE		DATE MADE	
SIZE OF CANDLES		WAX TOTAL	
NUMBER OF CANDLES		FRAGRANCE TOTAL	
ROOM TEMPERATURE		FRAGRANCE PERCENTAGE	

WAX	AMOUNTS	VENDOR / BATCH #
○		
○		
○		
○		
○		
○		
○		
○		
○		

FRAGRANCE	VANILLIN?	AMOUNTS	VENDOR / BATCH #
○	○ Y ○ N		
○	○ Y ○ N		
○	○ Y ○ N		
○	○ Y ○ N		
○	○ Y ○ N		
○	○ Y ○ N		
○	○ Y ○ N		
○	○ Y ○ N		

JAR / VESSEL / MOLD	WIDTH	HEIGHT
VENDOR		

WICK	QUANTITY	HEIGHT
VENDOR		

COLORANT	AMOUNTS	VENDOR / BATCH #
○		
○		
○		
○		
○		
○		

ACTIVITIES	AMOUNTS	VENDOR / BATCH #
○		
○		
○		
○		
○		
○		

THE WAX IS HEATED TO WHAT TEMPERATURE?	
THE FRAGRANCE IS ADDED AT WHAT TEMPERATURE?	
THE FRAGRANCE IS STIRRED IN THE WAX FOR HOW LONG?	
THE WAX IS POURED AT WHAT TEMPERATURE?	

NOTES

TEST BURN A

DATE		START TIME		END TIME	
ROOM SIZE		DAYS / WEEKS CURED			
CT	○ FAINT ○ DECENT ○ GOOD ○ GREAT ○ AMAZING			WICK TRIMMED	○ Y ○ N

OBSERVATIONS DURING THE FIRST BURN TEST

　

RESULTS AFTER THE BURN

　

HT	○ FAINT ○ DECENT ○ GOOD ○ GREAT ○ AMAZING	TOTAL BURN TIME	
WICK	○ OVER WICKED / TOO BIG ○ PROPERLY WICKED	○ UNDER WICKED / TOO SMALL	

TEST BURN B

DATE		START TIME		END TIME	
ROOM SIZE		DAYS / WEEKS CURED			
CT	○ FAINT ○ DECENT ○ GOOD ○ GREAT ○ AMAZING			WICK TRIMMED	○ Y ○ N

OBSERVATIONS DURING THE FIRST BURN TEST

　

RESULTS AFTER THE BURN

　

HT	○ FAINT ○ DECENT ○ GOOD ○ GREAT ○ AMAZING	TOTAL BURN TIME	
WICK	○ OVER WICKED / TOO BIG ○ PROPERLY WICKED	○ UNDER WICKED / TOO SMALL	

TEST BURN C

DATE		START TIME		END TIME	
ROOM SIZE		DAYS / WEEKS CURED			
CT	○ FAINT ○ DECENT ○ GOOD ○ GREAT ○ AMAZING			WICK TRIMMED	○ Y ○ N
OBSERVATIONS DURING THE FIRST BURN TEST					
RESULTS AFTER THE BURN					
HT	○ FAINT ○ DECENT ○ GOOD ○ GREAT ○ AMAZING			TOTAL BURN TIME	
WICK	○ OVER WICKED / TOO BIG		○ PROPERLY WICKED	○ UNDER WICKED / TOO SMALL	

TEST BURN D

DATE		START TIME		END TIME	
ROOM SIZE		DAYS / WEEKS CURED			
CT	○ FAINT ○ DECENT ○ GOOD ○ GREAT ○ AMAZING			WICK TRIMMED	○ Y ○ N
OBSERVATIONS DURING THE FIRST BURN TEST					
RESULTS AFTER THE BURN					
HT	○ FAINT ○ DECENT ○ GOOD ○ GREAT ○ AMAZING			TOTAL BURN TIME	
WICK	○ OVER WICKED / TOO BIG		○ PROPERLY WICKED	○ UNDER WICKED / TOO SMALL	

CANDLE CREATION LOG

DATE CREATED

CANDLE NAME

INGREDIENTS	AMOUNT	METHOD SUMMARY

OILS AND SCENTS	MOLD & FINISH

OVERALL RATING

○ 1   ○ 2   ○ 3   ○ 4   ○ 5   ○ 6   ○ 7   ○ 8   ○ 9   ○ 10

CANDLE MAKING LOGBOOK

DATE		BATCH	

NOTES

CANDLE TYPE

○ PILLAR	○ GEL
○ VOTIVE	○ CONTAINER TYPE: SIZE:
○ TART/MELT	○ OTHER

WAX TYPE

○ PARAFFIN	○ BEESWAX
○ SOY	○ GEL
○ PALM	○ OTHER

AMBIENT ROOM TEMP			
WAX BRAND			
QUANTITY			
MELT TEMP		POUR TEMP	
FRAGRANCE USED			
AMOUNT USED		POUR TEMP	
DYE TYPE		COLOR	
AMOUNT USED		TEMP ADDED	
WICK TYPE		SIZE	
CORE MATERIAL		# OF WICKS USED	
MOLD OR CONTAINER	○ MOLD ○ CONTAINER		
MOLD RELEASE USED	○ YES ○ NO		
WAS CONTAINER WARMED	○ YES ○ NO		
COOLING TIME		CURING TIME	

PROJECT		CREATED FOR			
DATE STARTED		DATE COMPLETED		RANK	/10
CANDLE TYPE	○ GLASSSES ○ JARS ○ OTHERS:				
WAX TYPE & BRAND		Q-TY			
POUR TEMP		MELT TEMP			
ADDITIVES USED					
SUPPLIES NEEDED					
COSTS					

INGREDIENTS	NAME / TYPE / BRAND	AMOUNT USED / SIZE	NOTES (TEMP/COLOR/ETC)
FRAGRANCE OIL			
DYE			
WICK			

AMBIENT ROOM TEMP		○ CONTAINER ○ MOLD		NUMBER OF POURS	
COOLING TIME		FINAL PRODUCT THROW	1 2 3 4 5	HOT THROW	1 2 3 4 5
MELT POOL		DIFFICULTY	○ EASY ○ MODERATE ○ CHALLENGING		

NOTES

CANDLE MAKING LOGBOOK

NAME OF CANDLE		DATE MADE	
SIZE OF CANDLES		WAX TOTAL	
NUMBER OF CANDLES		FRAGRANCE TOTAL	
ROOM TEMPERATURE		FRAGRANCE PERCENTAGE	

WAX	AMOUNTS	VENDOR / BATCH #
○		
○		
○		
○		
○		
○		
○		
○		
○		

FRAGRANCE	VANILLIN?	AMOUNTS	VENDOR / BATCH #
○	○ Y ○ N		
○	○ Y ○ N		
○	○ Y ○ N		
○	○ Y ○ N		
○	○ Y ○ N		
○	○ Y ○ N		
○	○ Y ○ N		
○	○ Y ○ N		

JAR / VESSEL / MOLD	WIDTH	HEIGHT

VENDOR	

WICK	QUANTITY	HEIGHT

VENDOR	

COLORANT	AMOUNTS	VENDOR / BATCH #
○		
○		
○		
○		
○		
○		

ACTIVITIES	AMOUNTS	VENDOR / BATCH #
○		
○		
○		
○		
○		
○		

THE WAX IS HEATED TO WHAT TEMPERATURE?	
THE FRAGRANCE IS ADDED AT WHAT TEMPERATURE?	
THE FRAGRANCE IS STIRRED IN THE WAX FOR HOW LONG?	
THE WAX IS POURED AT WHAT TEMPERATURE?	

NOTES

TEST BURN A

DATE		START TIME		END TIME		
ROOM SIZE		DAYS / WEEKS CURED				
CT	○ FAINT ○ DECENT ○ GOOD ○ GREAT ○ AMAZING			WICK TRIMMED		○ Y ○ N

OBSERVATIONS DURING THE FIRST BURN TEST

RESULTS AFTER THE BURN

HT	○ FAINT ○ DECENT ○ GOOD ○ GREAT ○ AMAZING	TOTAL BURN TIME	
WICK	○ OVER WICKED / TOO BIG ○ PROPERLY WICKED	○ UNDER WICKED / TOO SMALL	

TEST BURN B

DATE		START TIME		END TIME		
ROOM SIZE		DAYS / WEEKS CURED				
CT	○ FAINT ○ DECENT ○ GOOD ○ GREAT ○ AMAZING			WICK TRIMMED		○ Y ○ N

OBSERVATIONS DURING THE FIRST BURN TEST

RESULTS AFTER THE BURN

HT	○ FAINT ○ DECENT ○ GOOD ○ GREAT ○ AMAZING	TOTAL BURN TIME	
WICK	○ OVER WICKED / TOO BIG ○ PROPERLY WICKED	○ UNDER WICKED / TOO SMALL	

TEST BURN C

DATE		START TIME		END TIME	
ROOM SIZE		DAYS / WEEKS CURED			
CT	○ FAINT ○ DECENT ○ GOOD ○ GREAT ○ AMAZING			WICK TRIMMED	○ Y ○ N
OBSERVATIONS DURING THE FIRST BURN TEST					
RESULTS AFTER THE BURN					
HT	○ FAINT ○ DECENT ○ GOOD ○ GREAT ○ AMAZING			TOTAL BURN TIME	
WICK	○ OVER WICKED / TOO BIG		○ PROPERLY WICKED	○ UNDER WICKED / TOO SMALL	

TEST BURN D

DATE		START TIME		END TIME	
ROOM SIZE		DAYS / WEEKS CURED			
CT	○ FAINT ○ DECENT ○ GOOD ○ GREAT ○ AMAZING			WICK TRIMMED	○ Y ○ N
OBSERVATIONS DURING THE FIRST BURN TEST					
RESULTS AFTER THE BURN					
HT	○ FAINT ○ DECENT ○ GOOD ○ GREAT ○ AMAZING			TOTAL BURN TIME	
WICK	○ OVER WICKED / TOO BIG		○ PROPERLY WICKED	○ UNDER WICKED / TOO SMALL	

CANDLE CREATION LOG

DATE CREATED:

CANDLE NAME:

INGREDIENTS	AMOUNT	METHOD SUMMARY

OILS AND SCENTS	MOLD & FINISH

OVERALL RATING

○ 1 ○ 2 ○ 3 ○ 4 ○ 5 ○ 6 ○ 7 ○ 8 ○ 9 ○ 10

CANDLE MAKING LOGBOOK

DATE		BATCH	

NOTES

CANDLE TYPE

○ PILLAR	○ GEL
○ VOTIVE	○ CONTAINER TYPE: SIZE:
○ TART/MELT	○ OTHER

WAX TYPE

○ PARAFFIN	○ BEESWAX
○ SOY	○ GEL
○ PALM	○ OTHER

AMBIENT ROOM TEMP			
WAX BRAND			
QUANTITY			
MELT TEMP		POUR TEMP	
FRAGRANCE USED			
AMOUNT USED		POUR TEMP	
DYE TYPE		COLOR	
AMOUNT USED		TEMP ADDED	
WICK TYPE		SIZE	
CORE MATERIAL		# OF WICKS USED	
MOLD OR CONTAINER	○ MOLD ○ CONTAINER		
MOLD RELEASE USED	○ YES ○ NO		
WAS CONTAINER WARMED	○ YES ○ NO		
COOLING TIME		CURING TIME	

PROJECT		CREATED FOR			
DATE STARTED		DATE COMPLETED		RANK	/10
CANDLE TYPE	○ GLASSSES ○ JARS ○ OTHERS:				
WAX TYPE & BRAND		Q-TY			
POUR TEMP		MELT TEMP			
ADDITIVES USED					
SUPPLIES NEEDED					
COSTS					

INGREDIENTS	NAME / TYPE / BRAND	AMOUNT USED / SIZE	NOTES (TEMP/COLOR/ETC)
FRAGRANCE OIL			
DYE			
WICK			

AMBIENT ROOM TEMP		○ CONTAINER ○ MOLD		NUMBER OF POURS	
COOLING TIME		FINAL PRODUCT THROW	1 2 3 4 5	HOT THROW	1 2 3 4 5
MELT POOL		DIFFICULTY	○ EASY ○ MODERATE ○ CHALLENGING		
NOTES					

CANDLE MAKING LOGBOOK

NAME OF CANDLE		DATE MADE	
SIZE OF CANDLES		WAX TOTAL	
NUMBER OF CANDLES		FRAGRANCE TOTAL	
ROOM TEMPERATURE		FRAGRANCE PERCENTAGE	

WAX	AMOUNTS	VENDOR / BATCH #
○		
○		
○		
○		
○		
○		
○		
○		
○		
○		

FRAGRANCE	VANILLIN?	AMOUNTS	VENDOR / BATCH #
○	○ Y ○ N		
○	○ Y ○ N		
○	○ Y ○ N		
○	○ Y ○ N		
○	○ Y ○ N		
○	○ Y ○ N		
○	○ Y ○ N		
○	○ Y ○ N		

JAR / VESSEL / MOLD	WIDTH	HEIGHT
VENDOR		

WICK	QUANTITY	HEIGHT
VENDOR		

COLORANT	AMOUNTS	VENDOR / BATCH #
○		
○		
○		
○		
○		
○		

ACTIVITIES	AMOUNTS	VENDOR / BATCH #
○		
○		
○		
○		
○		
○		

THE WAX IS HEATED TO WHAT TEMPERATURE?	
THE FRAGRANCE IS ADDED AT WHAT TEMPERATURE?	
THE FRAGRANCE IS STIRRED IN THE WAX FOR HOW LONG?	
THE WAX IS POURED AT WHAT TEMPERATURE?	

NOTES

TEST BURN A

DATE		START TIME		END TIME	
ROOM SIZE		DAYS / WEEKS CURED			
CT	○ FAINT ○ DECENT ○ GOOD ○ GREAT ○ AMAZING			WICK TRIMMED	○ Y ○ N
OBSERVATIONS DURING THE FIRST BURN TEST					
RESULTS AFTER THE BURN					
HT	○ FAINT ○ DECENT ○ GOOD ○ GREAT ○ AMAZING			TOTAL BURN TIME	
WICK	○ OVER WICKED / TOO BIG		○ PROPERLY WICKED	○ UNDER WICKED / TOO SMALL	

TEST BURN B

DATE		START TIME		END TIME	
ROOM SIZE		DAYS / WEEKS CURED			
CT	○ FAINT ○ DECENT ○ GOOD ○ GREAT ○ AMAZING			WICK TRIMMED	○ Y ○ N
OBSERVATIONS DURING THE FIRST BURN TEST					
RESULTS AFTER THE BURN					
HT	○ FAINT ○ DECENT ○ GOOD ○ GREAT ○ AMAZING			TOTAL BURN TIME	
WICK	○ OVER WICKED / TOO BIG		○ PROPERLY WICKED	○ UNDER WICKED / TOO SMALL	

TEST BURN C

DATE		START TIME		END TIME	
ROOM SIZE		DAYS / WEEKS CURED			
CT	○ FAINT ○ DECENT ○ GOOD ○ GREAT ○ AMAZING			WICK TRIMMED	○ Y ○ N
OBSERVATIONS DURING THE FIRST BURN TEST					
RESULTS AFTER THE BURN					
HT	○ FAINT ○ DECENT ○ GOOD ○ GREAT ○ AMAZING			TOTAL BURN TIME	
WICK	○ OVER WICKED / TOO BIG		○ PROPERLY WICKED	○ UNDER WICKED / TOO SMALL	

TEST BURN D

DATE		START TIME		END TIME	
ROOM SIZE		DAYS / WEEKS CURED			
CT	○ FAINT ○ DECENT ○ GOOD ○ GREAT ○ AMAZING			WICK TRIMMED	○ Y ○ N
OBSERVATIONS DURING THE FIRST BURN TEST					
RESULTS AFTER THE BURN					
HT	○ FAINT ○ DECENT ○ GOOD ○ GREAT ○ AMAZING			TOTAL BURN TIME	
WICK	○ OVER WICKED / TOO BIG		○ PROPERLY WICKED	○ UNDER WICKED / TOO SMALL	

CANDLE CREATION LOG

DATE CREATED

CANDLE NAME

INGREDIENTS	AMOUNT	METHOD SUMMARY

OILS AND SCENTS	MOLD & FINISH

OVERALL RATING

○ 1 ○ 2 ○ 3 ○ 4 ○ 5 ○ 6 ○ 7 ○ 8 ○ 9 ○ 10

CANDLE MAKING LOGBOOK

DATE		BATCH	

NOTES

CANDLE TYPE

○ PILLAR	○ GEL
○ VOTIVE	○ CONTAINER TYPE: SIZE:
○ TART/MELT	○ OTHER

WAX TYPE

○ PARAFFIN	○ BEESWAX
○ SOY	○ GEL
○ PALM	○ OTHER

AMBIENT ROOM TEMP			
WAX BRAND			
QUANTITY			
MELT TEMP		POUR TEMP	
FRAGRANCE USED			
AMOUNT USED		POUR TEMP	
DYE TYPE		COLOR	
AMOUNT USED		TEMP ADDED	
WICK TYPE		SIZE	
CORE MATERIAL		# OF WICKS USED	
MOLD OR CONTAINER	○ MOLD ○ CONTAINER		
MOLD RELEASE USED	○ YES ○ NO		
WAS CONTAINER WARMED	○ YES ○ NO		
COOLING TIME		CURING TIME	

PROJECT		CREATED FOR			
DATE STARTED		DATE COMPLETED		RANK	/10
CANDLE TYPE	○ GLASSSES ○ JARS ○ OTHERS:				
WAX TYPE & BRAND		Q-TY			
POUR TEMP		MELT TEMP			
ADDITIVES USED					
SUPPLIES NEEDED					
COSTS					

INGREDIENTS	NAME / TYPE / BRAND	AMOUNT USED / SIZE	NOTES (TEMP/COLOR/ETC)
FRAGRANCE OIL			
DYE			
WICK			

AMBIENT ROOM TEMP		○ CONTAINER ○ MOLD		NUMBER OF POURS	
COOLING TIME		FINAL PRODUCT THROW	1 2 3 4 5	HOT THROW	1 2 3 4 5
MELT POOL		DIFFICULTY	○ EASY ○ MODERATE ○ CHALLENGING		
NOTES					

CANDLE MAKING LOGBOOK

NAME OF CANDLE		DATE MADE	
SIZE OF CANDLES		WAX TOTAL	
NUMBER OF CANDLES		FRAGRANCE TOTAL	
ROOM TEMPERATURE		FRAGRANCE PERCENTAGE	

WAX	AMOUNTS	VENDOR / BATCH #
○		
○		
○		
○		
○		
○		
○		
○		
○		

FRAGRANCE	VANILLIN?	AMOUNTS	VENDOR / BATCH #
○	○ Y ○ N		
○	○ Y ○ N		
○	○ Y ○ N		
○	○ Y ○ N		
○	○ Y ○ N		
○	○ Y ○ N		
○	○ Y ○ N		
○	○ Y ○ N		

JAR / VESSEL / MOLD	WIDTH	HEIGHT
VENDOR		

WICK	QUANTITY	HEIGHT
VENDOR		

COLORANT	AMOUNTS	VENDOR / BATCH #
○		
○		
○		
○		
○		
○		

ACTIVITIES	AMOUNTS	VENDOR / BATCH #
○		
○		
○		
○		
○		
○		

THE WAX IS HEATED TO WHAT TEMPERATURE?	
THE FRAGRANCE IS ADDED AT WHAT TEMPERATURE?	
THE FRAGRANCE IS STIRRED IN THE WAX FOR HOW LONG?	
THE WAX IS POURED AT WHAT TEMPERATURE?	

NOTES

TEST BURN A

DATE		START TIME		END TIME		
ROOM SIZE		DAYS / WEEKS CURED				
CT	○ FAINT ○ DECENT ○ GOOD ○ GREAT ○ AMAZING			WICK TRIMMED		○ Y ○ N

OBSERVATIONS DURING THE FIRST BURN TEST

RESULTS AFTER THE BURN

HT	○ FAINT ○ DECENT ○ GOOD ○ GREAT ○ AMAZING	TOTAL BURN TIME	
WICK	○ OVER WICKED / TOO BIG ○ PROPERLY WICKED	○ UNDER WICKED / TOO SMALL	

TEST BURN B

DATE		START TIME		END TIME		
ROOM SIZE		DAYS / WEEKS CURED				
CT	○ FAINT ○ DECENT ○ GOOD ○ GREAT ○ AMAZING			WICK TRIMMED		○ Y ○ N

OBSERVATIONS DURING THE FIRST BURN TEST

RESULTS AFTER THE BURN

HT	○ FAINT ○ DECENT ○ GOOD ○ GREAT ○ AMAZING	TOTAL BURN TIME	
WICK	○ OVER WICKED / TOO BIG ○ PROPERLY WICKED	○ UNDER WICKED / TOO SMALL	

TEST BURN C

DATE		START TIME		END TIME	
ROOM SIZE		DAYS / WEEKS CURED			
CT	○ FAINT ○ DECENT ○ GOOD ○ GREAT ○ AMAZING			WICK TRIMMED	○ Y ○ N

OBSERVATIONS DURING THE FIRST BURN TEST

RESULTS AFTER THE BURN

HT	○ FAINT ○ DECENT ○ GOOD ○ GREAT ○ AMAZING		TOTAL BURN TIME	
WICK	○ OVER WICKED / TOO BIG	○ PROPERLY WICKED	○ UNDER WICKED / TOO SMALL	

TEST BURN D

DATE		START TIME		END TIME	
ROOM SIZE		DAYS / WEEKS CURED			
CT	○ FAINT ○ DECENT ○ GOOD ○ GREAT ○ AMAZING			WICK TRIMMED	○ Y ○ N

OBSERVATIONS DURING THE FIRST BURN TEST

RESULTS AFTER THE BURN

HT	○ FAINT ○ DECENT ○ GOOD ○ GREAT ○ AMAZING		TOTAL BURN TIME	
WICK	○ OVER WICKED / TOO BIG	○ PROPERLY WICKED	○ UNDER WICKED / TOO SMALL	

CANDLE CREATION LOG

DATE CREATED

CANDLE NAME

INGREDIENTS	AMOUNT	METHOD SUMMARY

OILS AND SCENTS	MOLD & FINISH

OVERALL RATING

○ 1　○ 2　○ 3　○ 4　○ 5　○ 6　○ 7　○ 8　○ 9　○ 10

CANDLE MAKING LOGBOOK

DATE		BATCH	

NOTES			

CANDLE TYPE				
○ PILLAR		○ GEL		
○ VOTIVE		○ CONTAINER	TYPE:	SIZE:
○ TART/MELT		○ OTHER		

WAX TYPE		
○ PARAFFIN		○ BEESWAX
○ SOY		○ GEL
○ PALM		○ OTHER

AMBIENT ROOM TEMP			
WAX BRAND			
QUANTITY			
MELT TEMP		POUR TEMP	

FRAGRANCE USED			
AMOUNT USED		POUR TEMP	
DYE TYPE		COLOR	
AMOUNT USED		TEMP ADDED	
WICK TYPE		SIZE	
CORE MATERIAL		# OF WICKS USED	
MOLD OR CONTAINER	○ MOLD ○ CONTAINER		
MOLD RELEASE USED	○ YES ○ NO		
WAS CONTAINER WARMED	○ YES ○ NO		
COOLING TIME		CURING TIME	

PROJECT		CREATED FOR			
DATE STARTED		DATE COMPLETED		RANK	/10
CANDLE TYPE	○ GLASSSES ○ JARS ○ OTHERS:				
WAX TYPE & BRAND		Q-TY			
POUR TEMP		MELT TEMP			
ADDITIVES USED					
SUPPLIES NEEDED					
COSTS					

INGREDIENTS	NAME / TYPE / BRAND	AMOUNT USED / SIZE	NOTES (TEMP/COLOR/ETC)
FRAGRANCE OIL			
DYE			
WICK			

AMBIENT ROOM TEMP		○ CONTAINER ○ MOLD		NUMBER OF POURS	
COOLING TIME		FINAL PRODUCT THROW	1 2 3 4 5	HOT THROW	1 2 3 4 5
MELT POOL		DIFFICULTY	○ EASY ○ MODERATE ○ CHALLENGING		
NOTES					

CANDLE MAKING LOGBOOK

NAME OF CANDLE		DATE MADE	
SIZE OF CANDLES		WAX TOTAL	
NUMBER OF CANDLES		FRAGRANCE TOTAL	
ROOM TEMPERATURE		FRAGRANCE PERCENTAGE	

WAX	AMOUNTS	VENDOR / BATCH #
○		
○		
○		
○		
○		
○		
○		
○		
○		
○		

FRAGRANCE	VANILLIN?	AMOUNTS	VENDOR / BATCH #
○	○ Y ○ N		
○	○ Y ○ N		
○	○ Y ○ N		
○	○ Y ○ N		
○	○ Y ○ N		
○	○ Y ○ N		
○	○ Y ○ N		
○	○ Y ○ N		

JAR / VESSEL / MOLD	WIDTH	HEIGHT
VENDOR		

WICK	QUANTITY	HEIGHT
VENDOR		

COLORANT	AMOUNTS	VENDOR / BATCH #
○		
○		
○		
○		
○		
○		

ACTIVITIES	AMOUNTS	VENDOR / BATCH #
○		
○		
○		
○		
○		
○		

THE WAX IS HEATED TO WHAT TEMPERATURE?	
THE FRAGRANCE IS ADDED AT WHAT TEMPERATURE?	
THE FRAGRANCE IS STIRRED IN THE WAX FOR HOW LONG?	
THE WAX IS POURED AT WHAT TEMPERATURE?	

NOTES

TEST BURN A

DATE		START TIME		END TIME	
ROOM SIZE		DAYS / WEEKS CURED			
CT	○ FAINT ○ DECENT ○ GOOD ○ GREAT ○ AMAZING			WICK TRIMMED	○ Y ○ N

OBSERVATIONS DURING THE FIRST BURN TEST

RESULTS AFTER THE BURN

HT	○ FAINT ○ DECENT ○ GOOD ○ GREAT ○ AMAZING	TOTAL BURN TIME	
WICK	○ OVER WICKED / TOO BIG ○ PROPERLY WICKED		○ UNDER WICKED / TOO SMALL

TEST BURN B

DATE		START TIME		END TIME	
ROOM SIZE		DAYS / WEEKS CURED			
CT	○ FAINT ○ DECENT ○ GOOD ○ GREAT ○ AMAZING			WICK TRIMMED	○ Y ○ N

OBSERVATIONS DURING THE FIRST BURN TEST

RESULTS AFTER THE BURN

HT	○ FAINT ○ DECENT ○ GOOD ○ GREAT ○ AMAZING	TOTAL BURN TIME	
WICK	○ OVER WICKED / TOO BIG ○ PROPERLY WICKED		○ UNDER WICKED / TOO SMALL

TEST BURN C

DATE		START TIME		END TIME	
ROOM SIZE		DAYS / WEEKS CURED			
CT	○ FAINT ○ DECENT ○ GOOD ○ GREAT ○ AMAZING			WICK TRIMMED	○ Y ○ N

OBSERVATIONS DURING THE FIRST BURN TEST

RESULTS AFTER THE BURN

HT	○ FAINT ○ DECENT ○ GOOD ○ GREAT ○ AMAZING	TOTAL BURN TIME	
WICK	○ OVER WICKED / TOO BIG ○ PROPERLY WICKED ○ UNDER WICKED / TOO SMALL		

TEST BURN D

DATE		START TIME		END TIME	
ROOM SIZE		DAYS / WEEKS CURED			
CT	○ FAINT ○ DECENT ○ GOOD ○ GREAT ○ AMAZING			WICK TRIMMED	○ Y ○ N

OBSERVATIONS DURING THE FIRST BURN TEST

RESULTS AFTER THE BURN

HT	○ FAINT ○ DECENT ○ GOOD ○ GREAT ○ AMAZING	TOTAL BURN TIME	
WICK	○ OVER WICKED / TOO BIG ○ PROPERLY WICKED ○ UNDER WICKED / TOO SMALL		

CANDLE CREATION LOG

DATE CREATED

CANDLE NAME

INGREDIENTS	AMOUNT	METHOD SUMMARY

OILS AND SCENTS	MOLD & FINISH

OVERALL RATING

○ 1 ○ 2 ○ 3 ○ 4 ○ 5 ○ 6 ○ 7 ○ 8 ○ 9 ○ 10

CANDLE MAKING LOGBOOK

DATE		BATCH	

NOTES

CANDLE TYPE

○ PILLAR	○ GEL
○ VOTIVE	○ CONTAINER TYPE: SIZE:
○ TART/MELT	○ OTHER

WAX TYPE

○ PARAFFIN	○ BEESWAX
○ SOY	○ GEL
○ PALM	○ OTHER

AMBIENT ROOM TEMP			
WAX BRAND			
QUANTITY			
MELT TEMP		POUR TEMP	
FRAGRANCE USED			
AMOUNT USED		POUR TEMP	
DYE TYPE		COLOR	
AMOUNT USED		TEMP ADDED	
WICK TYPE		SIZE	
CORE MATERIAL		# OF WICKS USED	
MOLD OR CONTAINER	○ MOLD ○ CONTAINER		
MOLD RELEASE USED	○ YES ○ NO		
WAS CONTAINER WARMED	○ YES ○ NO		
COOLING TIME		CURING TIME	

PROJECT		CREATED FOR			
DATE STARTED		DATE COMPLETED		RANK	/10
CANDLE TYPE	○ GLASSSES ○ JARS ○ OTHERS:				
WAX TYPE & BRAND		Q-TY			
POUR TEMP		MELT TEMP			
ADDITIVES USED					
SUPPLIES NEEDED					
COSTS					

INGREDIENTS	NAME / TYPE / BRAND	AMOUNT USED / SIZE	NOTES (TEMP/COLOR/ETC)
FRAGRANCE OIL			
DYE			
WICK			

AMBIENT ROOM TEMP		○ CONTAINER ○ MOLD		NUMBER OF POURS	
COOLING TIME		FINAL PRODUCT THROW	1 2 3 4 5	HOT THROW	1 2 3 4 5
MELT POOL		DIFFICULTY	○ EASY ○ MODERATE ○ CHALLENGING		

NOTES

CANDLE MAKING LOGBOOK

NAME OF CANDLE		DATE MADE	
SIZE OF CANDLES		WAX TOTAL	
NUMBER OF CANDLES		FRAGRANCE TOTAL	
ROOM TEMPERATURE		FRAGRANCE PERCENTAGE	

WAX	AMOUNTS	VENDOR / BATCH #
○		
○		
○		
○		
○		
○		
○		
○		
○		
○		

FRAGRANCE	VANILLIN?	AMOUNTS	VENDOR / BATCH #
○	○ Y ○ N		
○	○ Y ○ N		
○	○ Y ○ N		
○	○ Y ○ N		
○	○ Y ○ N		
○	○ Y ○ N		
○	○ Y ○ N		
○	○ Y ○ N		

JAR / VESSEL / MOLD	WIDTH	HEIGHT
VENDOR		

WICK	QUANTITY	HEIGHT
VENDOR		

COLORANT	AMOUNTS	VENDOR / BATCH #
○		
○		
○		
○		
○		
○		

ACTIVITIES	AMOUNTS	VENDOR / BATCH #
○		
○		
○		
○		
○		
○		

THE WAX IS HEATED TO WHAT TEMPERATURE?	
THE FRAGRANCE IS ADDED AT WHAT TEMPERATURE?	
THE FRAGRANCE IS STIRRED IN THE WAX FOR HOW LONG?	
THE WAX IS POURED AT WHAT TEMPERATURE?	

NOTES

TEST BURN A

DATE		START TIME		END TIME	
ROOM SIZE		DAYS / WEEKS CURED			
CT	○ FAINT ○ DECENT ○ GOOD ○ GREAT ○ AMAZING			WICK TRIMMED	○ Y ○ N

OBSERVATIONS DURING THE FIRST BURN TEST

RESULTS AFTER THE BURN

HT	○ FAINT ○ DECENT ○ GOOD ○ GREAT ○ AMAZING	TOTAL BURN TIME	
WICK	○ OVER WICKED / TOO BIG ○ PROPERLY WICKED	○ UNDER WICKED / TOO SMALL	

TEST BURN B

DATE		START TIME		END TIME	
ROOM SIZE		DAYS / WEEKS CURED			
CT	○ FAINT ○ DECENT ○ GOOD ○ GREAT ○ AMAZING			WICK TRIMMED	○ Y ○ N

OBSERVATIONS DURING THE FIRST BURN TEST

RESULTS AFTER THE BURN

HT	○ FAINT ○ DECENT ○ GOOD ○ GREAT ○ AMAZING	TOTAL BURN TIME	
WICK	○ OVER WICKED / TOO BIG ○ PROPERLY WICKED	○ UNDER WICKED / TOO SMALL	

TEST BURN C

DATE		START TIME		END TIME	
ROOM SIZE		DAYS / WEEKS CURED			
CT	○ FAINT ○ DECENT ○ GOOD ○ GREAT ○ AMAZING			WICK TRIMMED	○ Y ○ N

OBSERVATIONS DURING THE FIRST BURN TEST

RESULTS AFTER THE BURN

HT	○ FAINT ○ DECENT ○ GOOD ○ GREAT ○ AMAZING	TOTAL BURN TIME	
WICK	○ OVER WICKED / TOO BIG ○ PROPERLY WICKED ○ UNDER WICKED / TOO SMALL		

TEST BURN D

DATE		START TIME		END TIME	
ROOM SIZE		DAYS / WEEKS CURED			
CT	○ FAINT ○ DECENT ○ GOOD ○ GREAT ○ AMAZING			WICK TRIMMED	○ Y ○ N

OBSERVATIONS DURING THE FIRST BURN TEST

RESULTS AFTER THE BURN

HT	○ FAINT ○ DECENT ○ GOOD ○ GREAT ○ AMAZING	TOTAL BURN TIME	
WICK	○ OVER WICKED / TOO BIG ○ PROPERLY WICKED ○ UNDER WICKED / TOO SMALL		

CANDLE CREATION LOG

DATE CREATED

CANDLE NAME

INGREDIENTS	AMOUNT	METHOD SUMMARY

OILS AND SCENTS	MOLD & FINISH

OVERALL RATING

○ 1 ○ 2 ○ 3 ○ 4 ○ 5 ○ 6 ○ 7 ○ 8 ○ 9 ○ 10

CANDLE MAKING LOGBOOK

DATE		BATCH	

NOTES

CANDLE TYPE

○ PILLAR	○ GEL
○ VOTIVE	○ CONTAINER TYPE: SIZE:
○ TART/MELT	○ OTHER

WAX TYPE

○ PARAFFIN	○ BEESWAX
○ SOY	○ GEL
○ PALM	○ OTHER

AMBIENT ROOM TEMP	
WAX BRAND	
QUANTITY	

MELT TEMP		POUR TEMP	

FRAGRANCE USED	

AMOUNT USED		POUR TEMP	
DYE TYPE		COLOR	
AMOUNT USED		TEMP ADDED	
WICK TYPE		SIZE	
CORE MATERIAL		# OF WICKS USED	

MOLD OR CONTAINER	○ MOLD ○ CONTAINER
MOLD RELEASE USED	○ YES ○ NO
WAS CONTAINER WARMED	○ YES ○ NO

COOLING TIME		CURING TIME	

PROJECT		CREATED FOR			
DATE STARTED		DATE COMPLETED		RANK	/10
CANDLE TYPE	○ GLASSSES ○ JARS ○ OTHERS:				
WAX TYPE & BRAND		Q-TY			
POUR TEMP		MELT TEMP			
ADDITIVES USED					
SUPPLIES NEEDED					
COSTS					

INGREDIENTS	NAME / TYPE / BRAND	AMOUNT USED / SIZE	NOTES (TEMP/COLOR/ETC)
FRAGRANCE OIL			
DYE			
WICK			

AMBIENT ROOM TEMP		○ CONTAINER ○ MOLD		NUMBER OF POURS	
COOLING TIME		FINAL PRODUCT THROW	1 2 3 4 5	HOT THROW	1 2 3 4 5
MELT POOL		DIFFICULTY	○ EASY ○ MODERATE ○ CHALLENGING		

NOTES

CANDLE MAKING LOGBOOK

NAME OF CANDLE		DATE MADE	
SIZE OF CANDLES		WAX TOTAL	
NUMBER OF CANDLES		FRAGRANCE TOTAL	
ROOM TEMPERATURE		FRAGRANCE PERCENTAGE	

WAX	AMOUNTS	VENDOR / BATCH #
○		
○		
○		
○		
○		
○		
○		
○		
○		
○		

FRAGRANCE	VANILLIN?	AMOUNTS	VENDOR / BATCH #
○	○ Y ○ N		
○	○ Y ○ N		
○	○ Y ○ N		
○	○ Y ○ N		
○	○ Y ○ N		
○	○ Y ○ N		
○	○ Y ○ N		
○	○ Y ○ N		

JAR / VESSEL / MOLD	WIDTH	HEIGHT
VENDOR		

WICK	QUANTITY	HEIGHT
VENDOR		

COLORANT	AMOUNTS	VENDOR / BATCH #
○		
○		
○		
○		
○		
○		

ACTIVITIES	AMOUNTS	VENDOR / BATCH #
○		
○		
○		
○		
○		
○		

THE WAX IS HEATED TO WHAT TEMPERATURE?	
THE FRAGRANCE IS ADDED AT WHAT TEMPERATURE?	
THE FRAGRANCE IS STIRRED IN THE WAX FOR HOW LONG?	
THE WAX IS POURED AT WHAT TEMPERATURE?	

NOTES

TEST BURN A

DATE		START TIME		END TIME	
ROOM SIZE		DAYS / WEEKS CURED			
CT	○ FAINT ○ DECENT ○ GOOD ○ GREAT ○ AMAZING			WICK TRIMMED	○ Y ○ N

OBSERVATIONS DURING THE FIRST BURN TEST

RESULTS AFTER THE BURN

HT	○ FAINT ○ DECENT ○ GOOD ○ GREAT ○ AMAZING		TOTAL BURN TIME	
WICK	○ OVER WICKED / TOO BIG	○ PROPERLY WICKED	○ UNDER WICKED / TOO SMALL	

TEST BURN B

DATE		START TIME		END TIME	
ROOM SIZE		DAYS / WEEKS CURED			
CT	○ FAINT ○ DECENT ○ GOOD ○ GREAT ○ AMAZING			WICK TRIMMED	○ Y ○ N

OBSERVATIONS DURING THE FIRST BURN TEST

RESULTS AFTER THE BURN

HT	○ FAINT ○ DECENT ○ GOOD ○ GREAT ○ AMAZING		TOTAL BURN TIME	
WICK	○ OVER WICKED / TOO BIG	○ PROPERLY WICKED	○ UNDER WICKED / TOO SMALL	

TEST BURN C

DATE		START TIME		END TIME	
ROOM SIZE		DAYS / WEEKS CURED			
CT	○ FAINT ○ DECENT ○ GOOD ○ GREAT ○ AMAZING			WICK TRIMMED	○ Y ○ N
OBSERVATIONS DURING THE FIRST BURN TEST					
RESULTS AFTER THE BURN					
HT	○ FAINT ○ DECENT ○ GOOD ○ GREAT ○ AMAZING			TOTAL BURN TIME	
WICK	○ OVER WICKED / TOO BIG		○ PROPERLY WICKED	○ UNDER WICKED / TOO SMALL	

TEST BURN D

DATE		START TIME		END TIME	
ROOM SIZE		DAYS / WEEKS CURED			
CT	○ FAINT ○ DECENT ○ GOOD ○ GREAT ○ AMAZING			WICK TRIMMED	○ Y ○ N
OBSERVATIONS DURING THE FIRST BURN TEST					
RESULTS AFTER THE BURN					
HT	○ FAINT ○ DECENT ○ GOOD ○ GREAT ○ AMAZING			TOTAL BURN TIME	
WICK	○ OVER WICKED / TOO BIG		○ PROPERLY WICKED	○ UNDER WICKED / TOO SMALL	

CANDLE CREATION LOG

DATE CREATED

CANDLE NAME

INGREDIENTS	AMOUNT	METHOD SUMMARY

OILS AND SCENTS	MOLD & FINISH

OVERALL RATING

○ 1 ○ 2 ○ 3 ○ 4 ○ 5 ○ 6 ○ 7 ○ 8 ○ 9 ○ 10

CANDLE MAKING LOGBOOK

DATE		BATCH	

NOTES

CANDLE TYPE

○ PILLAR	○ GEL
○ VOTIVE	○ CONTAINER TYPE: SIZE:
○ TART/MELT	○ OTHER

WAX TYPE

○ PARAFFIN	○ BEESWAX
○ SOY	○ GEL
○ PALM	○ OTHER

AMBIENT ROOM TEMP			
WAX BRAND			
QUANTITY			
MELT TEMP		POUR TEMP	
FRAGRANCE USED			
AMOUNT USED		POUR TEMP	
DYE TYPE		COLOR	
AMOUNT USED		TEMP ADDED	
WICK TYPE		SIZE	
CORE MATERIAL		# OF WICKS USED	
MOLD OR CONTAINER	○ MOLD ○ CONTAINER		
MOLD RELEASE USED	○ YES ○ NO		
WAS CONTAINER WARMED	○ YES ○ NO		
COOLING TIME		CURING TIME	

PROJECT		**CREATED FOR**			
DATE STARTED		**DATE COMPLETED**		**RANK**	/10
CANDLE TYPE	○ GLASSSES ○ JARS ○ OTHERS:				
WAX TYPE & BRAND		**Q-TY**			
POUR TEMP		**MELT TEMP**			
ADDITIVES USED					
SUPPLIES NEEDED					
COSTS					

INGREDIENTS	**NAME / TYPE / BRAND**	**AMOUNT USED / SIZE**	**NOTES** (TEMP/COLOR/ETC)
FRAGRANCE OIL			
DYE			
WICK			

AMBIENT ROOM TEMP		○ CONTAINER ○ MOLD		**NUMBER OF POURS**	
COOLING TIME		**FINAL PRODUCT THROW**	1 2 3 4 5	**HOT THROW**	1 2 3 4 5
MELT POOL		**DIFFICULTY**	○ EASY ○ MODERATE ○ CHALLENGING		

NOTES

CANDLE MAKING LOGBOOK

NAME OF CANDLE		DATE MADE	
SIZE OF CANDLES		WAX TOTAL	
NUMBER OF CANDLES		FRAGRANCE TOTAL	
ROOM TEMPERATURE		FRAGRANCE PERCENTAGE	

WAX	AMOUNTS	VENDOR / BATCH #
○		
○		
○		
○		
○		
○		
○		
○		
○		
○		

FRAGRANCE	VANILLIN?	AMOUNTS	VENDOR / BATCH #
○	○ Y ○ N		
○	○ Y ○ N		
○	○ Y ○ N		
○	○ Y ○ N		
○	○ Y ○ N		
○	○ Y ○ N		
○	○ Y ○ N		
○	○ Y ○ N		

JAR / VESSEL / MOLD	WIDTH	HEIGHT

VENDOR		

WICK	QUANTITY	HEIGHT

VENDOR		

COLORANT	AMOUNTS	VENDOR / BATCH #
○		
○		
○		
○		
○		
○		

ACTIVITIES	AMOUNTS	VENDOR / BATCH #
○		
○		
○		
○		
○		
○		

THE WAX IS HEATED TO WHAT TEMPERATURE?	
THE FRAGRANCE IS ADDED AT WHAT TEMPERATURE?	
THE FRAGRANCE IS STIRRED IN THE WAX FOR HOW LONG?	
THE WAX IS POURED AT WHAT TEMPERATURE?	

NOTES

TEST BURN A

DATE		START TIME		END TIME	
ROOM SIZE		DAYS / WEEKS CURED			
CT	○ FAINT ○ DECENT ○ GOOD ○ GREAT ○ AMAZING			**WICK TRIMMED**	○ Y ○ N

OBSERVATIONS DURING THE FIRST BURN TEST

RESULTS AFTER THE BURN

HT	○ FAINT ○ DECENT ○ GOOD ○ GREAT ○ AMAZING		**TOTAL BURN TIME**	
WICK	○ OVER WICKED / TOO BIG	○ PROPERLY WICKED	○ UNDER WICKED / TOO SMALL	

TEST BURN B

DATE		START TIME		END TIME	
ROOM SIZE		DAYS / WEEKS CURED			
CT	○ FAINT ○ DECENT ○ GOOD ○ GREAT ○ AMAZING			**WICK TRIMMED**	○ Y ○ N

OBSERVATIONS DURING THE FIRST BURN TEST

RESULTS AFTER THE BURN

HT	○ FAINT ○ DECENT ○ GOOD ○ GREAT ○ AMAZING		**TOTAL BURN TIME**	
WICK	○ OVER WICKED / TOO BIG	○ PROPERLY WICKED	○ UNDER WICKED / TOO SMALL	

TEST BURN C

DATE		START TIME		END TIME	
ROOM SIZE		DAYS / WEEKS CURED			
CT	○ FAINT ○ DECENT ○ GOOD ○ GREAT ○ AMAZING			WICK TRIMMED	○ Y ○ N

OBSERVATIONS DURING THE FIRST BURN TEST

_____
_____
_____
_____

RESULTS AFTER THE BURN

_____
_____
_____
_____

HT	○ FAINT ○ DECENT ○ GOOD ○ GREAT ○ AMAZING	TOTAL BURN TIME	
WICK	○ OVER WICKED / TOO BIG ○ PROPERLY WICKED ○ UNDER WICKED / TOO SMALL		

TEST BURN D

DATE		START TIME		END TIME	
ROOM SIZE		DAYS / WEEKS CURED			
CT	○ FAINT ○ DECENT ○ GOOD ○ GREAT ○ AMAZING			WICK TRIMMED	○ Y ○ N

OBSERVATIONS DURING THE FIRST BURN TEST

_____
_____
_____
_____

RESULTS AFTER THE BURN

_____
_____
_____
_____

HT	○ FAINT ○ DECENT ○ GOOD ○ GREAT ○ AMAZING	TOTAL BURN TIME	
WICK	○ OVER WICKED / TOO BIG ○ PROPERLY WICKED ○ UNDER WICKED / TOO SMALL		

CANDLE CREATION LOG

DATE CREATED

CANDLE NAME

INGREDIENTS	AMOUNT	METHOD SUMMARY

OILS AND SCENTS	MOLD & FINISH

OVERALL RATING

○ 1 ○ 2 ○ 3 ○ 4 ○ 5 ○ 6 ○ 7 ○ 8 ○ 9 ○ 10

CANDLE MAKING LOGBOOK

DATE		BATCH	
NOTES			

CANDLE TYPE				
○ PILLAR		○ GEL		
○ VOTIVE		○ CONTAINER	TYPE:	SIZE:
○ TART/MELT		○ OTHER		

WAX TYPE	
○ PARAFFIN	○ BEESWAX
○ SOY	○ GEL
○ PALM	○ OTHER

AMBIENT ROOM TEMP			
WAX BRAND			
QUANTITY			
MELT TEMP		POUR TEMP	

FRAGRANCE USED			
AMOUNT USED		POUR TEMP	
DYE TYPE		COLOR	
AMOUNT USED		TEMP ADDED	
WICK TYPE		SIZE	
CORE MATERIAL		# OF WICKS USED	

MOLD OR CONTAINER	○ MOLD ○ CONTAINER		
MOLD RELEASE USED	○ YES ○ NO		
WAS CONTAINER WARMED	○ YES ○ NO		
COOLING TIME		CURING TIME	

PROJECT		CREATED FOR			
DATE STARTED		DATE COMPLETED		RANK	/10
CANDLE TYPE	○ GLASSSES ○ JARS ○ OTHERS:				
WAX TYPE & BRAND		Q-TY			
POUR TEMP		MELT TEMP			
ADDITIVES USED					
SUPPLIES NEEDED					
COSTS					

INGREDIENTS	NAME / TYPE / BRAND	AMOUNT USED / SIZE	NOTES (TEMP/COLOR/ETC)
FRAGRANCE OIL			
DYE			
WICK			

AMBIENT ROOM TEMP		○ CONTAINER ○ MOLD		NUMBER OF POURS	
COOLING TIME		FINAL PRODUCT THROW	1 2 3 4 5	HOT THROW	1 2 3 4 5
MELT POOL		DIFFICULTY	○ EASY ○ MODERATE ○ CHALLENGING		
NOTES					

CANDLE MAKING LOGBOOK

NAME OF CANDLE		DATE MADE	
SIZE OF CANDLES		WAX TOTAL	
NUMBER OF CANDLES		FRAGRANCE TOTAL	
ROOM TEMPERATURE		FRAGRANCE PERCENTAGE	

WAX	AMOUNTS	VENDOR / BATCH #
○		
○		
○		
○		
○		
○		
○		
○		
○		
○		

FRAGRANCE	VANILLIN?	AMOUNTS	VENDOR / BATCH #
○	○ Y ○ N		
○	○ Y ○ N		
○	○ Y ○ N		
○	○ Y ○ N		
○	○ Y ○ N		
○	○ Y ○ N		
○	○ Y ○ N		
○	○ Y ○ N		

JAR / VESSEL / MOLD	WIDTH	HEIGHT
VENDOR		

WICK	QUANTITY	HEIGHT
VENDOR		

COLORANT	AMOUNTS	VENDOR / BATCH #
○		
○		
○		
○		
○		
○		

ACTIVITIES	AMOUNTS	VENDOR / BATCH #
○		
○		
○		
○		
○		
○		

THE WAX IS HEATED TO WHAT TEMPERATURE?	
THE FRAGRANCE IS ADDED AT WHAT TEMPERATURE?	
THE FRAGRANCE IS STIRRED IN THE WAX FOR HOW LONG?	
THE WAX IS POURED AT WHAT TEMPERATURE?	

NOTES

TEST BURN A

DATE		START TIME		END TIME	
ROOM SIZE		DAYS / WEEKS CURED			
CT	○ FAINT ○ DECENT ○ GOOD ○ GREAT ○ AMAZING			WICK TRIMMED	○ Y ○ N

OBSERVATIONS DURING THE FIRST BURN TEST

RESULTS AFTER THE BURN

HT	○ FAINT ○ DECENT ○ GOOD ○ GREAT ○ AMAZING	TOTAL BURN TIME	
WICK	○ OVER WICKED / TOO BIG ○ PROPERLY WICKED ○ UNDER WICKED / TOO SMALL		

TEST BURN B

DATE		START TIME		END TIME	
ROOM SIZE		DAYS / WEEKS CURED			
CT	○ FAINT ○ DECENT ○ GOOD ○ GREAT ○ AMAZING			WICK TRIMMED	○ Y ○ N

OBSERVATIONS DURING THE FIRST BURN TEST

RESULTS AFTER THE BURN

HT	○ FAINT ○ DECENT ○ GOOD ○ GREAT ○ AMAZING	TOTAL BURN TIME	
WICK	○ OVER WICKED / TOO BIG ○ PROPERLY WICKED ○ UNDER WICKED / TOO SMALL		

TEST BURN C

DATE		START TIME		END TIME	
ROOM SIZE		DAYS / WEEKS CURED			
CT	○ FAINT ○ DECENT ○ GOOD ○ GREAT ○ AMAZING			WICK TRIMMED	○ Y ○ N
OBSERVATIONS DURING THE FIRST BURN TEST					
RESULTS AFTER THE BURN					
HT	○ FAINT ○ DECENT ○ GOOD ○ GREAT ○ AMAZING			TOTAL BURN TIME	
WICK	○ OVER WICKED / TOO BIG		○ PROPERLY WICKED	○ UNDER WICKED / TOO SMALL	

TEST BURN D

DATE		START TIME		END TIME	
ROOM SIZE		DAYS / WEEKS CURED			
CT	○ FAINT ○ DECENT ○ GOOD ○ GREAT ○ AMAZING			WICK TRIMMED	○ Y ○ N
OBSERVATIONS DURING THE FIRST BURN TEST					
RESULTS AFTER THE BURN					
HT	○ FAINT ○ DECENT ○ GOOD ○ GREAT ○ AMAZING			TOTAL BURN TIME	
WICK	○ OVER WICKED / TOO BIG		○ PROPERLY WICKED	○ UNDER WICKED / TOO SMALL	

CANDLE CREATION LOG

DATE CREATED

CANDLE NAME

INGREDIENTS	AMOUNT	METHOD SUMMARY

OILS AND SCENTS	MOLD & FINISH

OVERALL RATING

○ 1   ○ 2   ○ 3   ○ 4   ○ 5   ○ 6   ○ 7   ○ 8   ○ 9   ○ 10

CANDLE MAKING LOGBOOK

DATE		BATCH	

NOTES	

CANDLE TYPE

○ PILLAR	○ GEL	
○ VOTIVE	○ CONTAINER TYPE:	SIZE:
○ TART/MELT	○ OTHER	

WAX TYPE

○ PARAFFIN	○ BEESWAX
○ SOY	○ GEL
○ PALM	○ OTHER

AMBIENT ROOM TEMP			
WAX BRAND			
QUANTITY			
MELT TEMP		POUR TEMP	
FRAGRANCE USED			
AMOUNT USED		POUR TEMP	
DYE TYPE		COLOR	
AMOUNT USED		TEMP ADDED	
WICK TYPE		SIZE	
CORE MATERIAL		# OF WICKS USED	
MOLD OR CONTAINER	○ MOLD ○ CONTAINER		
MOLD RELEASE USED	○ YES ○ NO		
WAS CONTAINER WARMED	○ YES ○ NO		
COOLING TIME		CURING TIME	

PROJECT		CREATED FOR			
DATE STARTED		DATE COMPLETED		RANK	/10
CANDLE TYPE	○ GLASSSES ○ JARS ○ OTHERS:				
WAX TYPE & BRAND		Q-TY			
POUR TEMP		MELT TEMP			
ADDITIVES USED					
SUPPLIES NEEDED					
COSTS					

INGREDIENTS	NAME / TYPE / BRAND	AMOUNT USED / SIZE	NOTES (TEMP/COLOR/ETC)
FRAGRANCE OIL			
DYE			
WICK			

AMBIENT ROOM TEMP		○ CONTAINER ○ MOLD		NUMBER OF POURS	
COOLING TIME		FINAL PRODUCT THROW	1 2 3 4 5	HOT THROW	1 2 3 4 5
MELT POOL		DIFFICULTY	○ EASY ○ MODERATE ○ CHALLENGING		

NOTES

CANDLE MAKING LOGBOOK

NAME OF CANDLE		DATE MADE	
SIZE OF CANDLES		WAX TOTAL	
NUMBER OF CANDLES		FRAGRANCE TOTAL	
ROOM TEMPERATURE		FRAGRANCE PERCENTAGE	

WAX	AMOUNTS	VENDOR / BATCH #

FRAGRANCE	VANILLIN?	AMOUNTS	VENDOR / BATCH #
	○ Y ○ N		
	○ Y ○ N		
	○ Y ○ N		
	○ Y ○ N		
	○ Y ○ N		
	○ Y ○ N		
	○ Y ○ N		
	○ Y ○ N		

JAR / VESSEL / MOLD	WIDTH	HEIGHT
VENDOR		

WICK	QUANTITY	HEIGHT
VENDOR		

COLORANT	AMOUNTS	VENDOR / BATCH #
○		
○		
○		
○		
○		
○		

ACTIVITIES	AMOUNTS	VENDOR / BATCH #
○		
○		
○		
○		
○		
○		

THE WAX IS HEATED TO WHAT TEMPERATURE?	
THE FRAGRANCE IS ADDED AT WHAT TEMPERATURE?	
THE FRAGRANCE IS STIRRED IN THE WAX FOR HOW LONG?	
THE WAX IS POURED AT WHAT TEMPERATURE?	

NOTES

TEST BURN A

DATE		START TIME		END TIME	
ROOM SIZE		DAYS / WEEKS CURED			
CT	○ FAINT ○ DECENT ○ GOOD ○ GREAT ○ AMAZING			WICK TRIMMED	○ Y ○ N

OBSERVATIONS DURING THE FIRST BURN TEST

RESULTS AFTER THE BURN

HT	○ FAINT ○ DECENT ○ GOOD ○ GREAT ○ AMAZING		TOTAL BURN TIME	
WICK	○ OVER WICKED / TOO BIG	○ PROPERLY WICKED	○ UNDER WICKED / TOO SMALL	

TEST BURN B

DATE		START TIME		END TIME	
ROOM SIZE		DAYS / WEEKS CURED			
CT	○ FAINT ○ DECENT ○ GOOD ○ GREAT ○ AMAZING			WICK TRIMMED	○ Y ○ N

OBSERVATIONS DURING THE FIRST BURN TEST

RESULTS AFTER THE BURN

HT	○ FAINT ○ DECENT ○ GOOD ○ GREAT ○ AMAZING		TOTAL BURN TIME	
WICK	○ OVER WICKED / TOO BIG	○ PROPERLY WICKED	○ UNDER WICKED / TOO SMALL	

TEST BURN C

DATE		START TIME		END TIME	
ROOM SIZE		DAYS / WEEKS CURED			
CT	○ FAINT ○ DECENT ○ GOOD ○ GREAT ○ AMAZING			WICK TRIMMED	○ Y ○ N

OBSERVATIONS DURING THE FIRST BURN TEST

RESULTS AFTER THE BURN

HT	○ FAINT ○ DECENT ○ GOOD ○ GREAT ○ AMAZING		TOTAL BURN TIME	
WICK	○ OVER WICKED / TOO BIG	○ PROPERLY WICKED	○ UNDER WICKED / TOO SMALL	

TEST BURN D

DATE		START TIME		END TIME	
ROOM SIZE		DAYS / WEEKS CURED			
CT	○ FAINT ○ DECENT ○ GOOD ○ GREAT ○ AMAZING			WICK TRIMMED	○ Y ○ N

OBSERVATIONS DURING THE FIRST BURN TEST

RESULTS AFTER THE BURN

HT	○ FAINT ○ DECENT ○ GOOD ○ GREAT ○ AMAZING		TOTAL BURN TIME	
WICK	○ OVER WICKED / TOO BIG	○ PROPERLY WICKED	○ UNDER WICKED / TOO SMALL	

CANDLE CREATION LOG

DATE CREATED

CANDLE NAME

INGREDIENTS	AMOUNT	METHOD SUMMARY

OILS AND SCENTS | **MOLD & FINISH**

OVERALL RATING

○ 1 ○ 2 ○ 3 ○ 4 ○ 5 ○ 6 ○ 7 ○ 8 ○ 9 ○ 10

CANDLE MAKING LOGBOOK

DATE		BATCH	
NOTES			

CANDLE TYPE

○ PILLAR	○ GEL
○ VOTIVE	○ CONTAINER TYPE: SIZE:
○ TART/MELT	○ OTHER

WAX TYPE

○ PARAFFIN	○ BEESWAX
○ SOY	○ GEL
○ PALM	○ OTHER

AMBIENT ROOM TEMP			
WAX BRAND			
QUANTITY			
MELT TEMP		POUR TEMP	
FRAGRANCE USED			
AMOUNT USED		POUR TEMP	
DYE TYPE		COLOR	
AMOUNT USED		TEMP ADDED	
WICK TYPE		SIZE	
CORE MATERIAL		# OF WICKS USED	
MOLD OR CONTAINER	○ MOLD ○ CONTAINER		
MOLD RELEASE USED	○ YES ○ NO		
WAS CONTAINER WARMED	○ YES ○ NO		
COOLING TIME		CURING TIME	

PROJECT		CREATED FOR			
DATE STARTED		DATE COMPLETED		RANK	/10
CANDLE TYPE	○ GLASSSES ○ JARS ○ OTHERS:				
WAX TYPE & BRAND		Q-TY			
POUR TEMP		MELT TEMP			
ADDITIVES USED					
SUPPLIES NEEDED					
COSTS					

INGREDIENTS	NAME / TYPE / BRAND	AMOUNT USED / SIZE	NOTES (TEMP/COLOR/ETC)
FRAGRANCE OIL			
DYE			
WICK			

AMBIENT ROOM TEMP		○ CONTAINER ○ MOLD		NUMBER OF POURS	
COOLING TIME		FINAL PRODUCT THROW	1 2 3 4 5	HOT THROW	1 2 3 4 5
MELT POOL		DIFFICULTY	○ EASY ○ MODERATE ○ CHALLENGING		
NOTES					

CANDLE MAKING LOGBOOK

NAME OF CANDLE		DATE MADE	
SIZE OF CANDLES		WAX TOTAL	
NUMBER OF CANDLES		FRAGRANCE TOTAL	
ROOM TEMPERATURE		FRAGRANCE PERCENTAGE	

WAX	AMOUNTS	VENDOR / BATCH #
○		
○		
○		
○		
○		
○		
○		
○		
○		

FRAGRANCE	VANILLIN?	AMOUNTS	VENDOR / BATCH #
○	○ Y ○ N		
○	○ Y ○ N		
○	○ Y ○ N		
○	○ Y ○ N		
○	○ Y ○ N		
○	○ Y ○ N		
○	○ Y ○ N		
○	○ Y ○ N		

JAR / VESSEL / MOLD	WIDTH	HEIGHT
VENDOR		

WICK	QUANTITY	HEIGHT
VENDOR		

COLORANT	AMOUNTS	VENDOR / BATCH #
○		
○		
○		
○		
○		
○		

ACTIVITIES	AMOUNTS	VENDOR / BATCH #
○		
○		
○		
○		
○		
○		

THE WAX IS HEATED TO WHAT TEMPERATURE?	
THE FRAGRANCE IS ADDED AT WHAT TEMPERATURE?	
THE FRAGRANCE IS STIRRED IN THE WAX FOR HOW LONG?	
THE WAX IS POURED AT WHAT TEMPERATURE?	

NOTES

TEST BURN A

DATE		START TIME		END TIME	
ROOM SIZE		DAYS / WEEKS CURED			
CT	○ FAINT ○ DECENT ○ GOOD ○ GREAT ○ AMAZING			WICK TRIMMED	○ Y ○ N

OBSERVATIONS DURING THE FIRST BURN TEST

RESULTS AFTER THE BURN

HT	○ FAINT ○ DECENT ○ GOOD ○ GREAT ○ AMAZING	TOTAL BURN TIME	
WICK	○ OVER WICKED / TOO BIG ○ PROPERLY WICKED		○ UNDER WICKED / TOO SMALL

TEST BURN B

DATE		START TIME		END TIME	
ROOM SIZE		DAYS / WEEKS CURED			
CT	○ FAINT ○ DECENT ○ GOOD ○ GREAT ○ AMAZING			WICK TRIMMED	○ Y ○ N

OBSERVATIONS DURING THE FIRST BURN TEST

RESULTS AFTER THE BURN

HT	○ FAINT ○ DECENT ○ GOOD ○ GREAT ○ AMAZING	TOTAL BURN TIME	
WICK	○ OVER WICKED / TOO BIG ○ PROPERLY WICKED		○ UNDER WICKED / TOO SMALL

TEST BURN C

DATE		START TIME		END TIME	
ROOM SIZE		DAYS / WEEKS CURED			
CT	○ FAINT ○ DECENT ○ GOOD ○ GREAT ○ AMAZING			WICK TRIMMED	○ Y ○ N

OBSERVATIONS DURING THE FIRST BURN TEST

RESULTS AFTER THE BURN

HT	○ FAINT ○ DECENT ○ GOOD ○ GREAT ○ AMAZING	TOTAL BURN TIME	
WICK	○ OVER WICKED / TOO BIG ○ PROPERLY WICKED ○ UNDER WICKED / TOO SMALL		

TEST BURN D

DATE		START TIME		END TIME	
ROOM SIZE		DAYS / WEEKS CURED			
CT	○ FAINT ○ DECENT ○ GOOD ○ GREAT ○ AMAZING			WICK TRIMMED	○ Y ○ N

OBSERVATIONS DURING THE FIRST BURN TEST

RESULTS AFTER THE BURN

HT	○ FAINT ○ DECENT ○ GOOD ○ GREAT ○ AMAZING	TOTAL BURN TIME	
WICK	○ OVER WICKED / TOO BIG ○ PROPERLY WICKED ○ UNDER WICKED / TOO SMALL		

CANDLE CREATION LOG

DATE CREATED

CANDLE NAME

INGREDIENTS	AMOUNT	METHOD SUMMARY

OILS AND SCENTS	MOLD & FINISH

OVERALL RATING

○ 1   ○ 2   ○ 3   ○ 4   ○ 5   ○ 6   ○ 7   ○ 8   ○ 9   ○ 10

CANDLE MAKING LOGBOOK

DATE		BATCH	
NOTES			

CANDLE TYPE				
○ PILLAR		○ GEL		
○ VOTIVE		○ CONTAINER	TYPE:	SIZE:
○ TART/MELT		○ OTHER		

WAX TYPE		
○ PARAFFIN	○ BEESWAX	
○ SOY	○ GEL	
○ PALM	○ OTHER	

AMBIENT ROOM TEMP			
WAX BRAND			
QUANTITY			
MELT TEMP		POUR TEMP	
FRAGRANCE USED			
AMOUNT USED		POUR TEMP	
DYE TYPE		COLOR	
AMOUNT USED		TEMP ADDED	
WICK TYPE		SIZE	
CORE MATERIAL		# OF WICKS USED	
MOLD OR CONTAINER	○ MOLD ○ CONTAINER		
MOLD RELEASE USED	○ YES ○ NO		
WAS CONTAINER WARMED	○ YES ○ NO		
COOLING TIME		CURING TIME	

PROJECT		CREATED FOR			
DATE STARTED		DATE COMPLETED		RANK	/10
CANDLE TYPE	○ GLASSSES ○ JARS ○ OTHERS:				
WAX TYPE & BRAND		Q-TY			
POUR TEMP		MELT TEMP			
ADDITIVES USED					
SUPPLIES NEEDED					
COSTS					

INGREDIENTS	NAME / TYPE / BRAND	AMOUNT USED / SIZE	NOTES (TEMP/COLOR/ETC)
FRAGRANCE OIL			
DYE			
WICK			

AMBIENT ROOM TEMP		○ CONTAINER ○ MOLD		NUMBER OF POURS	
COOLING TIME		FINAL PRODUCT THROW	1 2 3 4 5	HOT THROW	1 2 3 4 5
MELT POOL		DIFFICULTY	○ EASY ○ MODERATE ○ CHALLENGING		

NOTES

CANDLE MAKING LOGBOOK

NAME OF CANDLE		DATE MADE	
SIZE OF CANDLES		WAX TOTAL	
NUMBER OF CANDLES		FRAGRANCE TOTAL	
ROOM TEMPERATURE		FRAGRANCE PERCENTAGE	

WAX	AMOUNTS	VENDOR / BATCH #
○		
○		
○		
○		
○		
○		
○		
○		
○		
○		

FRAGRANCE	VANILLIN?	AMOUNTS	VENDOR / BATCH #
○	○ Y ○ N		
○	○ Y ○ N		
○	○ Y ○ N		
○	○ Y ○ N		
○	○ Y ○ N		
○	○ Y ○ N		
○	○ Y ○ N		
○	○ Y ○ N		

JAR / VESSEL / MOLD	WIDTH	HEIGHT
VENDOR		

WICK	QUANTITY	HEIGHT
VENDOR		

COLORANT	AMOUNTS	VENDOR / BATCH #
○		
○		
○		
○		
○		
○		

ACTIVITIES	AMOUNTS	VENDOR / BATCH #
○		
○		
○		
○		
○		
○		

THE WAX IS HEATED TO WHAT TEMPERATURE?	
THE FRAGRANCE IS ADDED AT WHAT TEMPERATURE?	
THE FRAGRANCE IS STIRRED IN THE WAX FOR HOW LONG?	
THE WAX IS POURED AT WHAT TEMPERATURE?	

NOTES

TEST BURN A

DATE		START TIME		END TIME	
ROOM SIZE		DAYS / WEEKS CURED			
CT	○ FAINT ○ DECENT ○ GOOD ○ GREAT ○ AMAZING			WICK TRIMMED	○ Y ○ N

OBSERVATIONS DURING THE FIRST BURN TEST

RESULTS AFTER THE BURN

HT	○ FAINT ○ DECENT ○ GOOD ○ GREAT ○ AMAZING		TOTAL BURN TIME	
WICK	○ OVER WICKED / TOO BIG	○ PROPERLY WICKED	○ UNDER WICKED / TOO SMALL	

TEST BURN B

DATE		START TIME		END TIME	
ROOM SIZE		DAYS / WEEKS CURED			
CT	○ FAINT ○ DECENT ○ GOOD ○ GREAT ○ AMAZING			WICK TRIMMED	○ Y ○ N

OBSERVATIONS DURING THE FIRST BURN TEST

RESULTS AFTER THE BURN

HT	○ FAINT ○ DECENT ○ GOOD ○ GREAT ○ AMAZING		TOTAL BURN TIME	
WICK	○ OVER WICKED / TOO BIG	○ PROPERLY WICKED	○ UNDER WICKED / TOO SMALL	

TEST BURN C

DATE		START TIME		END TIME	
ROOM SIZE		DAYS / WEEKS CURED			
CT	○ FAINT ○ DECENT ○ GOOD ○ GREAT ○ AMAZING			WICK TRIMMED	○ Y ○ N

OBSERVATIONS DURING THE FIRST BURN TEST

RESULTS AFTER THE BURN

HT	○ FAINT ○ DECENT ○ GOOD ○ GREAT ○ AMAZING	TOTAL BURN TIME	
WICK	○ OVER WICKED / TOO BIG ○ PROPERLY WICKED ○ UNDER WICKED / TOO SMALL		

TEST BURN D

DATE		START TIME		END TIME	
ROOM SIZE		DAYS / WEEKS CURED			
CT	○ FAINT ○ DECENT ○ GOOD ○ GREAT ○ AMAZING			WICK TRIMMED	○ Y ○ N

OBSERVATIONS DURING THE FIRST BURN TEST

RESULTS AFTER THE BURN

HT	○ FAINT ○ DECENT ○ GOOD ○ GREAT ○ AMAZING	TOTAL BURN TIME	
WICK	○ OVER WICKED / TOO BIG ○ PROPERLY WICKED ○ UNDER WICKED / TOO SMALL		

CANDLE CREATION LOG

DATE CREATED

CANDLE NAME

INGREDIENTS	AMOUNT	METHOD SUMMARY

OILS AND SCENTS	MOLD & FINISH

OVERALL RATING

○ 1 ○ 2 ○ 3 ○ 4 ○ 5 ○ 6 ○ 7 ○ 8 ○ 9 ○ 10

CANDLE MAKING LOGBOOK

DATE		BATCH	

NOTES	

CANDLE TYPE

○ PILLAR	○ GEL		
○ VOTIVE	○ CONTAINER	TYPE:	SIZE:
○ TART/MELT	○ OTHER		

WAX TYPE

○ PARAFFIN	○ BEESWAX
○ SOY	○ GEL
○ PALM	○ OTHER

AMBIENT ROOM TEMP			
WAX BRAND			
QUANTITY			
MELT TEMP		POUR TEMP	

FRAGRANCE USED			
AMOUNT USED		POUR TEMP	
DYE TYPE		COLOR	
AMOUNT USED		TEMP ADDED	
WICK TYPE		SIZE	
CORE MATERIAL		# OF WICKS USED	
MOLD OR CONTAINER	○ MOLD ○ CONTAINER		
MOLD RELEASE USED	○ YES ○ NO		
WAS CONTAINER WARMED	○ YES ○ NO		
COOLING TIME		CURING TIME	

PROJECT		CREATED FOR			
DATE STARTED		DATE COMPLETED		RANK	/10
CANDLE TYPE	○ GLASSSES ○ JARS ○ OTHERS:				
WAX TYPE & BRAND		Q-TY			
POUR TEMP		MELT TEMP			
ADDITIVES USED					
SUPPLIES NEEDED					
COSTS					

INGREDIENTS	NAME / TYPE / BRAND	AMOUNT USED / SIZE	NOTES (TEMP/COLOR/ETC)
FRAGRANCE OIL			
DYE			
WICK			

AMBIENT ROOM TEMP		○ CONTAINER ○ MOLD		NUMBER OF POURS	
COOLING TIME		FINAL PRODUCT THROW	1 2 3 4 5	HOT THROW	1 2 3 4 5
MELT POOL		DIFFICULTY	○ EASY ○ MODERATE ○ CHALLENGING		

NOTES

CANDLE MAKING LOGBOOK

NAME OF CANDLE		DATE MADE	
SIZE OF CANDLES		WAX TOTAL	
NUMBER OF CANDLES		FRAGRANCE TOTAL	
ROOM TEMPERATURE		FRAGRANCE PERCENTAGE	

WAX	AMOUNTS	VENDOR / BATCH #
○		
○		
○		
○		
○		
○		
○		
○		
○		
○		

FRAGRANCE	VANILLIN?	AMOUNTS	VENDOR / BATCH #
○	○ Y ○ N		
○	○ Y ○ N		
○	○ Y ○ N		
○	○ Y ○ N		
○	○ Y ○ N		
○	○ Y ○ N		
○	○ Y ○ N		
○	○ Y ○ N		

JAR / VESSEL / MOLD	WIDTH	HEIGHT
VENDOR		

WICK	QUANTITY	HEIGHT
VENDOR		

COLORANT	AMOUNTS	VENDOR / BATCH #
○		
○		
○		
○		
○		
○		

ACTIVITIES	AMOUNTS	VENDOR / BATCH #
○		
○		
○		
○		
○		
○		

THE WAX IS HEATED TO WHAT TEMPERATURE?	
THE FRAGRANCE IS ADDED AT WHAT TEMPERATURE?	
THE FRAGRANCE IS STIRRED IN THE WAX FOR HOW LONG?	
THE WAX IS POURED AT WHAT TEMPERATURE?	

NOTES

TEST BURN A

DATE		START TIME		END TIME	
ROOM SIZE		DAYS / WEEKS CURED			
CT	○ FAINT ○ DECENT ○ GOOD ○ GREAT ○ AMAZING			WICK TRIMMED	○ Y ○ N
OBSERVATIONS DURING THE FIRST BURN TEST					
RESULTS AFTER THE BURN					
HT	○ FAINT ○ DECENT ○ GOOD ○ GREAT ○ AMAZING			TOTAL BURN TIME	
WICK	○ OVER WICKED / TOO BIG		○ PROPERLY WICKED	○ UNDER WICKED / TOO SMALL	

TEST BURN B

DATE		START TIME		END TIME	
ROOM SIZE		DAYS / WEEKS CURED			
CT	○ FAINT ○ DECENT ○ GOOD ○ GREAT ○ AMAZING			WICK TRIMMED	○ Y ○ N
OBSERVATIONS DURING THE FIRST BURN TEST					
RESULTS AFTER THE BURN					
HT	○ FAINT ○ DECENT ○ GOOD ○ GREAT ○ AMAZING			TOTAL BURN TIME	
WICK	○ OVER WICKED / TOO BIG		○ PROPERLY WICKED	○ UNDER WICKED / TOO SMALL	

TEST BURN C

DATE		START TIME		END TIME	
ROOM SIZE		DAYS / WEEKS CURED			
CT	○ FAINT ○ DECENT ○ GOOD ○ GREAT ○ AMAZING			WICK TRIMMED	○ Y ○ N
OBSERVATIONS DURING THE FIRST BURN TEST					
RESULTS AFTER THE BURN					
HT	○ FAINT ○ DECENT ○ GOOD ○ GREAT ○ AMAZING			TOTAL BURN TIME	
WICK	○ OVER WICKED / TOO BIG		○ PROPERLY WICKED	○ UNDER WICKED / TOO SMALL	

TEST BURN D

DATE		START TIME		END TIME	
ROOM SIZE		DAYS / WEEKS CURED			
CT	○ FAINT ○ DECENT ○ GOOD ○ GREAT ○ AMAZING			WICK TRIMMED	○ Y ○ N
OBSERVATIONS DURING THE FIRST BURN TEST					
RESULTS AFTER THE BURN					
HT	○ FAINT ○ DECENT ○ GOOD ○ GREAT ○ AMAZING			TOTAL BURN TIME	
WICK	○ OVER WICKED / TOO BIG		○ PROPERLY WICKED	○ UNDER WICKED / TOO SMALL	

CANDLE CREATION LOG

DATE CREATED

CANDLE NAME

INGREDIENTS	AMOUNT	METHOD SUMMARY

OILS AND SCENTS	MOLD & FINISH

OVERALL RATING

○ 1   ○ 2   ○ 3   ○ 4   ○ 5   ○ 6   ○ 7   ○ 8   ○ 9   ○ 10

CANDLE MAKING LOGBOOK

DATE		BATCH	

NOTES

CANDLE TYPE

- ○ PILLAR
- ○ VOTIVE
- ○ TART/MELT
- ○ GEL
- ○ CONTAINER   TYPE: SIZE:
- ○ OTHER

WAX TYPE

- ○ PARAFFIN
- ○ SOY
- ○ PALM
- ○ BEESWAX
- ○ GEL
- ○ OTHER

AMBIENT ROOM TEMP			
WAX BRAND			
QUANTITY			
MELT TEMP		POUR TEMP	
FRAGRANCE USED			
AMOUNT USED		POUR TEMP	
DYE TYPE		COLOR	
AMOUNT USED		TEMP ADDED	
WICK TYPE		SIZE	
CORE MATERIAL		# OF WICKS USED	
MOLD OR CONTAINER	○ MOLD ○ CONTAINER		
MOLD RELEASE USED	○ YES ○ NO		
WAS CONTAINER WARMED	○ YES ○ NO		
COOLING TIME		CURING TIME	

PROJECT		CREATED FOR			
DATE STARTED		DATE COMPLETED		RANK	/10
CANDLE TYPE	○ GLASSSES ○ JARS ○ OTHERS:				
WAX TYPE & BRAND		Q-TY			
POUR TEMP		MELT TEMP			
ADDITIVES USED					
SUPPLIES NEEDED					
COSTS					

INGREDIENTS	NAME / TYPE / BRAND	AMOUNT USED / SIZE	NOTES (TEMP/COLOR/ETC)
FRAGRANCE OIL			
DYE			
WICK			

AMBIENT ROOM TEMP		○ CONTAINER ○ MOLD		NUMBER OF POURS	
COOLING TIME		FINAL PRODUCT THROW	1 2 3 4 5	HOT THROW	1 2 3 4 5
MELT POOL		DIFFICULTY	○ EASY ○ MODERATE ○ CHALLENGING		

NOTES

CANDLE MAKING LOGBOOK

NAME OF CANDLE		DATE MADE	
SIZE OF CANDLES		WAX TOTAL	
NUMBER OF CANDLES		FRAGRANCE TOTAL	
ROOM TEMPERATURE		FRAGRANCE PERCENTAGE	

WAX	AMOUNTS	VENDOR / BATCH #
○		
○		
○		
○		
○		
○		
○		
○		
○		

FRAGRANCE	VANILLIN?	AMOUNTS	VENDOR / BATCH #
○	○ Y ○ N		
○	○ Y ○ N		
○	○ Y ○ N		
○	○ Y ○ N		
○	○ Y ○ N		
○	○ Y ○ N		
○	○ Y ○ N		
○	○ Y ○ N		

JAR / VESSEL / MOLD	WIDTH	HEIGHT
VENDOR		

WICK	QUANTITY	HEIGHT
VENDOR		

COLORANT	AMOUNTS	VENDOR / BATCH #
○		
○		
○		
○		
○		
○		

ACTIVITIES	AMOUNTS	VENDOR / BATCH #
○		
○		
○		
○		
○		
○		

THE WAX IS HEATED TO WHAT TEMPERATURE?	
THE FRAGRANCE IS ADDED AT WHAT TEMPERATURE?	
THE FRAGRANCE IS STIRRED IN THE WAX FOR HOW LONG?	
THE WAX IS POURED AT WHAT TEMPERATURE?	

NOTES

TEST BURN A

DATE		START TIME		END TIME	
ROOM SIZE		DAYS / WEEKS CURED			
CT	○ FAINT ○ DECENT ○ GOOD ○ GREAT ○ AMAZING			WICK TRIMMED	○ Y ○ N

OBSERVATIONS DURING THE FIRST BURN TEST

RESULTS AFTER THE BURN

HT	○ FAINT ○ DECENT ○ GOOD ○ GREAT ○ AMAZING		TOTAL BURN TIME	
WICK	○ OVER WICKED / TOO BIG	○ PROPERLY WICKED	○ UNDER WICKED / TOO SMALL	

TEST BURN B

DATE		START TIME		END TIME	
ROOM SIZE		DAYS / WEEKS CURED			
CT	○ FAINT ○ DECENT ○ GOOD ○ GREAT ○ AMAZING			WICK TRIMMED	○ Y ○ N

OBSERVATIONS DURING THE FIRST BURN TEST

RESULTS AFTER THE BURN

HT	○ FAINT ○ DECENT ○ GOOD ○ GREAT ○ AMAZING		TOTAL BURN TIME	
WICK	○ OVER WICKED / TOO BIG	○ PROPERLY WICKED	○ UNDER WICKED / TOO SMALL	

TEST BURN C

DATE		START TIME		END TIME	
ROOM SIZE		DAYS / WEEKS CURED			
CT	○ FAINT ○ DECENT ○ GOOD ○ GREAT ○ AMAZING			WICK TRIMMED	○ Y ○ N

OBSERVATIONS DURING THE FIRST BURN TEST

RESULTS AFTER THE BURN

HT	○ FAINT ○ DECENT ○ GOOD ○ GREAT ○ AMAZING	TOTAL BURN TIME	
WICK	○ OVER WICKED / TOO BIG ○ PROPERLY WICKED ○ UNDER WICKED / TOO SMALL		

TEST BURN D

DATE		START TIME		END TIME	
ROOM SIZE		DAYS / WEEKS CURED			
CT	○ FAINT ○ DECENT ○ GOOD ○ GREAT ○ AMAZING			WICK TRIMMED	○ Y ○ N

OBSERVATIONS DURING THE FIRST BURN TEST

RESULTS AFTER THE BURN

HT	○ FAINT ○ DECENT ○ GOOD ○ GREAT ○ AMAZING	TOTAL BURN TIME	
WICK	○ OVER WICKED / TOO BIG ○ PROPERLY WICKED ○ UNDER WICKED / TOO SMALL		

CANDLE CREATION LOG

DATE CREATED

CANDLE NAME

INGREDIENTS	AMOUNT	METHOD SUMMARY

OILS AND SCENTS	MOLD & FINISH

OVERALL RATING

○ 1   ○ 2   ○ 3   ○ 4   ○ 5   ○ 6   ○ 7   ○ 8   ○ 9   ○ 10

CANDLE MAKING LOGBOOK

DATE		BATCH	

NOTES

CANDLE TYPE

○ PILLAR	○ GEL
○ VOTIVE	○ CONTAINER TYPE: SIZE:
○ TART/MELT	○ OTHER

WAX TYPE

○ PARAFFIN	○ BEESWAX
○ SOY	○ GEL
○ PALM	○ OTHER

AMBIENT ROOM TEMP	
WAX BRAND	
QUANTITY	

MELT TEMP		POUR TEMP	

FRAGRANCE USED	

AMOUNT USED		POUR TEMP	
DYE TYPE		COLOR	
AMOUNT USED		TEMP ADDED	
WICK TYPE		SIZE	
CORE MATERIAL		# OF WICKS USED	

MOLD OR CONTAINER	○ MOLD ○ CONTAINER
MOLD RELEASE USED	○ YES ○ NO
WAS CONTAINER WARMED	○ YES ○ NO

COOLING TIME		CURING TIME	

PROJECT		CREATED FOR			
DATE STARTED		DATE COMPLETED		RANK	/10
CANDLE TYPE	○ GLASSSES ○ JARS ○ OTHERS:				
WAX TYPE & BRAND		Q-TY			
POUR TEMP		MELT TEMP			
ADDITIVES USED					
SUPPLIES NEEDED					
COSTS					

INGREDIENTS	NAME / TYPE / BRAND	AMOUNT USED / SIZE	NOTES (TEMP/COLOR/ETC)
FRAGRANCE OIL			
DYE			
WICK			

AMBIENT ROOM TEMP		○ CONTAINER ○ MOLD		NUMBER OF POURS	
COOLING TIME		FINAL PRODUCT THROW	1 2 3 4 5	HOT THROW	1 2 3 4 5
MELT POOL		DIFFICULTY	○ EASY ○ MODERATE ○ CHALLENGING		
NOTES					

CANDLE MAKING LOGBOOK

NAME OF CANDLE		DATE MADE	
SIZE OF CANDLES		WAX TOTAL	
NUMBER OF CANDLES		FRAGRANCE TOTAL	
ROOM TEMPERATURE		FRAGRANCE PERCENTAGE	

WAX	AMOUNTS	VENDOR / BATCH #
○		
○		
○		
○		
○		
○		
○		
○		
○		
○		

FRAGRANCE	VANILLIN?	AMOUNTS	VENDOR / BATCH #
○	○ Y ○ N		
○	○ Y ○ N		
○	○ Y ○ N		
○	○ Y ○ N		
○	○ Y ○ N		
○	○ Y ○ N		
○	○ Y ○ N		
○	○ Y ○ N		

JAR / VESSEL / MOLD	WIDTH	HEIGHT
VENDOR		

WICK	QUANTITY	HEIGHT
VENDOR		

COLORANT	AMOUNTS	VENDOR / BATCH #
○		
○		
○		
○		
○		
○		

ACTIVITIES	AMOUNTS	VENDOR / BATCH #
○		
○		
○		
○		
○		
○		

THE WAX IS HEATED TO WHAT TEMPERATURE?	
THE FRAGRANCE IS ADDED AT WHAT TEMPERATURE?	
THE FRAGRANCE IS STIRRED IN THE WAX FOR HOW LONG?	
THE WAX IS POURED AT WHAT TEMPERATURE?	

NOTES

TEST BURN A

DATE		START TIME		END TIME	
ROOM SIZE		DAYS / WEEKS CURED			
CT	○ FAINT ○ DECENT ○ GOOD ○ GREAT ○ AMAZING			WICK TRIMMED	○ Y ○ N

OBSERVATIONS DURING THE FIRST BURN TEST

RESULTS AFTER THE BURN

HT	○ FAINT ○ DECENT ○ GOOD ○ GREAT ○ AMAZING	TOTAL BURN TIME	
WICK	○ OVER WICKED / TOO BIG ○ PROPERLY WICKED ○ UNDER WICKED / TOO SMALL		

TEST BURN B

DATE		START TIME		END TIME	
ROOM SIZE		DAYS / WEEKS CURED			
CT	○ FAINT ○ DECENT ○ GOOD ○ GREAT ○ AMAZING			WICK TRIMMED	○ Y ○ N

OBSERVATIONS DURING THE FIRST BURN TEST

RESULTS AFTER THE BURN

HT	○ FAINT ○ DECENT ○ GOOD ○ GREAT ○ AMAZING	TOTAL BURN TIME	
WICK	○ OVER WICKED / TOO BIG ○ PROPERLY WICKED ○ UNDER WICKED / TOO SMALL		

TEST BURN C

DATE		START TIME		END TIME		
ROOM SIZE		DAYS / WEEKS CURED				
CT	○ FAINT ○ DECENT ○ GOOD ○ GREAT ○ AMAZING			WICK TRIMMED		○ Y ○ N
OBSERVATIONS DURING THE FIRST BURN TEST						
RESULTS AFTER THE BURN						
HT	○ FAINT ○ DECENT ○ GOOD ○ GREAT ○ AMAZING			TOTAL BURN TIME		
WICK	○ OVER WICKED / TOO BIG		○ PROPERLY WICKED	○ UNDER WICKED / TOO SMALL		

TEST BURN D

DATE		START TIME		END TIME		
ROOM SIZE		DAYS / WEEKS CURED				
CT	○ FAINT ○ DECENT ○ GOOD ○ GREAT ○ AMAZING			WICK TRIMMED		○ Y ○ N
OBSERVATIONS DURING THE FIRST BURN TEST						
RESULTS AFTER THE BURN						
HT	○ FAINT ○ DECENT ○ GOOD ○ GREAT ○ AMAZING			TOTAL BURN TIME		
WICK	○ OVER WICKED / TOO BIG		○ PROPERLY WICKED	○ UNDER WICKED / TOO SMALL		

 Copyrights 2021 - All rights reserved

You may not reproduce, duplicate or send the contents of this book without direct written permission from the author. You cannot hereby despite any circumstance blame the publisher or hold him or her te legal responsibility for any reparation, compensation or monetary forfeiture owing to the information included herein, either in a direct or indirect way.

Legal Notice: This book has copyright protection. You can use the book for personal purpose. You should not sell, use, alter, distribute, quote, take excerpts or paraphrase in part of whole the material contained in this book without obtaining the permission of the author first.

Disclaimer Notice: You must take note that the information in this document is for casual reading and entertainment purpose only. We have made every attempt to provide accurate, up to date and reliable information. We do not express or imply guarantees of any kind. The person who read admit that the writer is not occupied in giving legal, financial, medical or other advice. We put this book content by sourcing various places. Please consult a licensed professional before you try any techniques shown in this book. By going through this document, the book lover comes to an agreement that under no situation is the author accountable for any forfeiture, direct or indirect, which they may incur because of the use of material contained in this document, including, but not limited to, - errors, omissions, or inaccuracies.

As a small family company, your feedback is very important to us.

Please let us know how you like our book at:

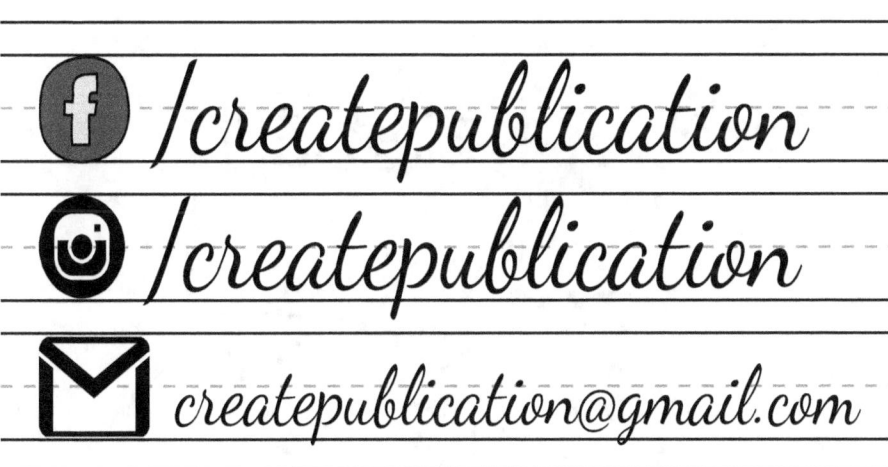

THIS BOOK BELONGS TO:

------

www.ingramcontent.com/pod-product-compliance
Lightning Source LLC
Chambersburg PA
CBHW071458070526
44578CB00001B/378